THE RELIGION OF JESUS
AND THE FAITH OF PAUL

THE RELIGION OF JESUS AND THE FAITH OF PAUL

*THE SELLY OAK LECTURES, 1923
ON THE COMMUNION OF JESUS WITH GOD
& THE COMMUNION OF PAUL WITH CHRIST*

BY

ADOLF DEISSMANN

D.THEOL. (MARBURG); D.D. (ABERDEEN, ST. ANDREW'S, MANCHESTER)
CORRESPONDING MEMBER OF THE ARCHÆOLOGICAL INSTITUTE OF THE GERMAN REICH
PROFESSOR OF THEOLOGY IN THE UNIVERSITY OF BERLIN

TRANSLATED BY

WILLIAM E. WILSON, B.D.

PROFESSOR OF NEW TESTAMENT THEOLOGY AND CHRISTIAN ETHICS
IN THE SELLY OAK COLLEGES, BIRMINGHAM

Wipf and Stock Publishers
EUGENE, OREGON

Wipf and Stock Publishers
199 West 8th Avenue, Suite 3
Eugene, Oregon 97401

The Religion of Jesus and the Faith of Paul
The Selly Oak Lectures, 1923 on the Communion of Jesus with God & the
Communion of Paul with Christ
By Deissmann, Adolf
ISBN: 1-59244-171-8
Publication date 3/6/2003
Previously published by George H. Doran Company, 1926

PREFACE

THESE lectures were delivered in February and March 1923 in the Weoley Hill Church, Selly Oak, at the invitation of the Selly Oak Colleges (Woodbrooke, Kingsmead, Westhill, Fircroft, and Carey Hall). They are now published without any essential alteration. I did not give the two courses one after the other, but alternating with one another; nevertheless they will be more easily understood if read as here printed, one after the other. As my *St. Paul* (Hodder & Stoughton, 1912) has long been out of print, I have in the Paul course taken over many passages from that book; this may serve as a substitute for the larger work until it is possible for me to publish a new edition of it.[1]

In looking back over my work in Selly Oak, my hearty thanks are due: to the

[1] New and Revised Edition, published Autumn 1926.

PREFACE

Senatus of the Selly Oak Colleges for their confidence and truly brotherly reception ; to the colleagues and students for their lively interest, which expressed itself in discussion after each lecture and to me indicated much stimulation of thought ; to the trusty helpers who worked with me so untiringly week by week in the study formerly used by my venerable friend Dr. Rendel Harris, where we felt the presence of beneficent spirits ; very specially to Professor William E. Wilson, my apt translator, who, from time to time, with assistance from Mrs. Johanna M. Powers, in a most interesting interchange of thought gave the lectures their English dress. The help of Miss Frances W. Naish was also of the greatest value to me.

The whole time in Selly Oak was under the blessing of a great word : in the Lectures and in daily intercourse it was a time of fellowship. This experience of fellowship from my British fellow-Christians came to me after the long night like the rosy finger of the dawn, and the old hymn of my ancestor Christian Knorr von Rosenroth " Morgenglanz der Ewigkeit," which we often sang together at Selly Oak out of the Fellowship Hymn Book in the translation of Jane Borthwick, gained for me a deep symbolical meaning:

> With the early morning rays
> Do Thou on our darkness shine,
> And dispel with purest light
> All our night

ADOLF DEISSMANN.

Berlin-Wilmersdorf,
  Prinzregentenstr. 6,
    Whitsuntide, 1923.

NOTE BY TRANSLATOR

THERE is no German edition of this book. My function as translator was much more intimate and personal than is that of one who renders a printed book out of one language into another. The privilege of the hours spent with Professor Deissmann when we gave his thought, expressed in German, the English dress presented in these lectures is one on which I shall always look back with the deepest pleasure. I know I am only expressing the feelings of all my colleagues at Selly Oak and of the students there in saying that we welcomed Dr. Deissmann as a great scholar and theologian, and that we parted from him as a great religious teacher and a personal friend.

WILLIAM E. WILSON.

Woodbrooke,
  June, 1923.

CONTENTS

	PAGE
PREFACE	5
NOTE BY TRANSLATOR	9

PART I

COMMUNION WITH GOD IN THE EXPERIENCE OF JESUS

LECTURE
I.	THE TASK, THE SOURCES AND THE METHOD	15
II.	THE PRAYER LIFE OF JESUS AS THE REFLEX OF HIS COMMUNION WITH GOD	43
III.	THE COMMUNION OF JESUS WITH GOD THE FATHER AND GOD THE LORD	69
IV.	THE WORKING OUT OF COMMUNION WITH GOD IN THE MESSAGE OF THE KINGDOM	101
V.	THE DYNAMIC CULMINATION OF COMMUNION WITH GOD IN JESUS' CONSCIOUSNESS OF MISSION AND MESSIAHSHIP. WHAT NEW THING DID JESUS BRING?	123

CONTENTS

PART II

COMMUNION WITH CHRIST IN THE EXPERIENCE OF PAUL

LECTURE

I. THE TASK, THE SOURCES AND THE METHOD. PRELIMINARY EXEGETICAL QUESTIONS . 153

II. THE BEGINNING AND ESSENTIAL NATURE OF COMMUNION WITH CHRIST . . . 181

III. SALVATION IN COMMUNION WITH CHRIST . 201

IV. THE NEW CREATION IN COMMUNION WITH CHRIST. THE FELLOWSHIP OF THE SUFFERINGS OF CHRIST . . . 222

V. CHRIST—MYSTICISM AND ETHICS. LATER DEVELOPMENTS FROM THE PAULINE COMMUNION WITH CHRIST 245

INDEX 279

PART I

THE COMMUNION OF JESUS WITH GOD

I

THE TASK, THE SOURCES AND THE METHOD

THE theme on which I am to speak to you is " Communion with God in the experience of Jesus." If we take this task seriously it means that we must penetrate into the last and greatest inner experiences of Jesus. We wish to take it seriously, but I must begin with the paradoxical statement that by historical means we cannot completely solve this problem. When we compare this task with the other, the investigation of " Communion with Christ in the experience of Paul," and when we look at it in itself, it appears to me, after deep thought, to be so difficult that I must say without hesitation it is not to be completely performed by historical means.

One who endeavours to reproduce an essential part of the inner life of the Apostle Paul is from the very first in a better position. He has sources to work with which are indeed fragmentary, but of which the fragments are genuine, and full of important matter. Pauline Letters are, from the very fact that they never were intended to be published, in the pure simplicity of their primitive character, perfect reflections of the personality of Paul. When we come to them, we experience the sense of distance from their author that smaller people discover when faced with a great personality. But we yet feel that we are not separated from him by an unbridgable gulf. Paul is still for us historically and psychologically so nearly approachable, that we can attempt the work without insuperable difficulty.

From Jesus, on the other hand, there has come to us not a single line of His own writing. The whole historical tradition about Him is indirect. It was, at the earliest, after He had gone that people began to collect remembrances of His first disciples and set down single sayings of His in writing. These certainly are not complete, but fragmentary, and we do not know the situation in which many words were spoken. Add to this, that the greater number of these sayings of Jesus are not personal confessions about His own inner life, but warnings, words of comfort, commands, gospel counsels, instructions for missionaries, prophecies, all addressed to the needs of others.

Taken all together, the Letters of Paul are truly human documents of a marvellous subjectivity, of a passionate inwardness, and in most cases we can reconstruct the situation with a vivid sense of reality. On the other hand, the words of Jesus which have come to us through tradition by other hands, are generally quite extraordinarily objective. The vibrations of His inner conflicts have seldom been preserved. The heroic passion of an activity of His will predominates through all. Even the remembrance of the *de profundis* hours, which are the very creative force for the inner man, and which, as Jesus developed, He probably experienced, has been lost.

A simile may help to make clear the contrast in means of approach to Paul and to Jesus : Behind a thick luxuriant primeval forest rises a distant chain of mountains with glittering, high peaks ! You can go into the wood—certainly not without trouble, but still step by step getting deeper into its mystery. But it is a daring feat to climb the chain of mountains. Be thankful if you can climb one hill, one peak. You will never walk upon the summit.

Considered as an historical theological problem, the elucidation of the spiritual experiences of Jesus in communion with God is finally insoluble. It seems to me to be the tragedy of historical theology, that it can never arrive at its last and greatest object by its own means. It is true that, in the historical investigation of any great personality of the past, the investigator is bound to come to the limits of his knowledge. But it may be objected : "Look at the enormous literature about Jesus! In the *bibliotheca Christiana* all the rooms are full of this literature, especially since the discovery of the historical method in the last few hundred years." I reply that the existence of this literature does not remove my difficulty. Certainly, hundreds upon hundreds in every land and in every church have written about Jesus, but we have often only done it as if we were walking, without knowing it, over precipices. Or in cases where we ought to have gone down to the very depths, we have rapidly skimmed the surface. The tragedy of those seems to be even greater who do not realise that they are actors in a tragedy, who deal with the problem as though they were writing of Tom, Dick or Harry, and think when they have put down on paper the " Teaching of Jesus " they have given us the Master Himself.

If I have begun my lecture with the paradox that the problem of the experience of Jesus is finally insoluble, it is only in order that we may estimate carefully our own inadequacy, and realise the necessity for modesty and care. This paradox must not make us resigned, it must not drive us into a fruitless agnosticism, but it must make clear to us the great difficulty, and must demonstrate to us that the historical investigator, with his historical instruments, has not the means of opening to us the last chamber.

I believe that there is a way to press on to a full understanding of Jesus, but it is not a way made by historical science. The way of historical science is narrow. If one wants truly to grasp Jesus, one must make the way broader. It is the way which Paul called " the more excellent way." " *Tantum Jesus cognoscitur, quantum diligitur* "—" Jesus is known as much as He is loved." I know, even when I begin an academic lecture on Jesus, that there is an unacademical way to Jesus, and that it is the best way, because it is open to all. Jesus lives not only in the historical sources of the Gospel, but is to be experienced by us also, wherever He is manifested in the present day, as living energy.

AND THE FAITH OF PAUL 21

There are periods in which He has manifested Himself more through tradition, and there are periods in which He has manifested Himself more through the revelation of this energy. It appears to me that we stand at the beginning of one of these latter periods.

What we have experienced in the last ten years seemed at first sight to be nothing but a *parousia* of anti-Christ, that left nothing but ruin, wretchedness, hunger, bitterness, hatred and darkness. But because it is a period of darkness and misery, we may trust that a new *parousia* of Jesus Himself has begun. Jesus, even when He wandered beneath the sun of His Galilean home, identified Himself with the hungry, the sick, the prisoners, and homeless fugitives. Now millions upon millions of hungry, sick prisoners and fugitives driven from home by brutal force, a great choir of the disinherited, sigh their troubles to heaven in Europe and Asia. There where this mass of wretched humanity is, Jesus Himself is present. There

He is in each individual of millions. He is hungry, He is sick, a prisoner, homeless.

And even if this mass of wretchedness continues for some time to come, yes, if through acts of brutal violence it is increased to-day and to-morrow, yet in many lands earnest and deep-thinking men have recognised in the stillness that He is hungry, sick, a prisoner, and homeless. And they have gone to Him in the least of His brethren and have helped them. So the people who have sat in darkness have perceived on the horizon the first gleams of the dawning of a new day for mankind.

Is it too fantastic to hope that after the night of distress of the present era a new day will follow—a time of new enthusiasm in following Jesus, and that by means of this very activity in following Jesus there will come a new revelation of Jesus Himself?

I have this hope; and therefore I am, though as an historian well aware of the limits of my knowledge and the relativity of my results, no pessimist in relation to the greatest of all questions : whether one can know Jesus. "*Tantum Jesus cognoscitur, quantum diligitur*"—"Jesus is known as much as He is loved."

Now, I believe it is important that one should not mix the two methods of looking at the matter. One must render to history the things that are history's, and to love the things that are love's. But in one and the same personality, the two methods of approach can undoubtedly unite. On one point there is, for the historian, a contact between his historical and his personal attitude to Jesus. Every historian who has more to do than merely investigate old texts, to solve chronological problems and make certain of outward facts, who rather has to deal with the soul of a great man, must in the end, if he wishes to gain an all-round picture, divine by means of intuition. This cannot happen without sympathetic imaginative entry into the life, without *Agape* (love). If anywhere, the Pauline saying applies to this kind of work, "knowledge puffeth up, but charity edifieth."

In the reconstruction of the picture of Jesus, the combining power will always be love. We can here, in an exceptional case, compare the Pauline *Agape* with the Platonic *Eros*. But the investigator must not trade too much with his *Eros*. He must not weaken the best part of the armour of his soul by talking too much about it. In occasional solemn hours of historical insight it may serve him as final interpreter. But everyday work must be done with the tools of the workshop.

Through what has been said, it will already have become clear that our task, which is only partly to be done by historical methods, is not identical with the study of what is usually called "The Teaching of Jesus." If that were our objective, the theme would be much easier. "The Teaching of Jesus" can be easily set forth, just because the tradition itself is relatively objective. But the teaching which is expressed outwardly is some-

AND THE FAITH OF PAUL 25

thing secondary. It points back to something primary, namely, inner communion with God. Our problem is not the secondary matter, but the primary : not the teaching, but the experience behind it.

Have you ever seen how they make bands of iron ? You may observe two chief stages. There is a point at which an unformed piece of glowing iron goes through the rolling-mill. Writhing like a fiery serpent, it comes out in the shape of a band, white-hot and glittering. Workmen then grasp it with tongs and lay it on the ground, where it gradually becomes cold and loses all its glow. At this point, the second stage has begun. The bands are tied together in bundles with wires, and carried on waggons to the dealers. Anybody then can take them in his hands, buy them by weight, and use them in house and stable.

The Teaching of Jesus, as we lay it up in store in our books, is like the iron bands which are sold all ready for use. But before that, these very bands were in the stage of white-hot, glittering metal. If we could succeed in transferring the words of Jesus back into this stage of white-hot blazing metal, then we could understand without difficulty His communion with God. On this point, again, it seems to me quite clear that extraordinary methods are required. The ordinary armoury of the study is not sufficient. It is the rare hours of solemn experience that help us here.— For instance, in the fiery furnace of affliction most of us have probably realised that some familiar word of Jesus has at last been revealed to us in its true meaning. In many respects the last ten years have been for science a time of decline. For the greatest and most delicate task of historical science, for the reproduction of the historical Jesus, they may mean an inspiration. I do not believe I am in error when I say that among all peoples, through the great trouble of this time, a refining and deepening of the understanding of the real personality of Jesus has come about.

Thus the two are connected : a new self-revelation of Jesus to us, and a new know-

AND THE FAITH OF PAUL 27

ledge concerning Jesus gained by us. He meets us again in millions of the least of His brethren, and we, having been better equipped than previous generations through the psychological experiences of our time, can perhaps reach Him better than was possible before.

* * *

What, then, are the sources where we can expect to find help towards the solution of the problem?

Jesus grew up in the retirement of a little country town in Galilee. About His development, tradition has preserved us nothing certain; scarcely more than that the veil lifts to tell us that His childhood was spent in a circle of numerous brothers and sisters, and that He was known as " the carpenter." [1]

[1] Compare the extremely interesting tradition in the Gospel of St. Mark, chap. 6, verse 3 : " Is not this the carpenter, the son of Mary, the brother of James, and Joses and of Juda and of Simon? And are not his sisters here with us?" It is very important to see here, that Jesus had four brothers and at the least

Apart from this, we have no materials in the words of the mature man that could enable us psychologically to reconstruct the experience of the adolescent. There is no development of Jesus during the time of His public activity to be discovered. The burning of His inner life, the lightning flash, the disappearance, and the lightning again of great personal certainties, the stages of His conflict with the official religious authorities—to set all that in a scheme of development, step by step, would be to treat prophecy like doctrine.

The very state of our sources ought to warn us against such dilettantism. We have not a line written by the hand of Jesus Himself. In the main, we must turn to the tradition which is recorded for us in the Gospels of Matthew, Mark and Luke. These

---

two sisters, and also that He was a manual labourer. But we do not know anything else about His childhood, except that wonderful story in St. Luke 2.: " and when he was twelve years old," and so on, which I think is historically well transmitted and very significant indeed for our theme.

sources offer but little towards a biography of the outer circumstances of Jesus—in fact, the chronological order of the incidents remains very uncertain : only in general we can guess that one section belongs more probably to the beginning of His official activity, another to the end.[1] The sources offer much towards the understanding of the most important matter, the inner life of Jesus, but here also it ought to be pointed out how fragmentary is the character of the tradition.

Jesus is greater than the tradition about Him. The tradition is only the last echo of His words. It is only the mirror of Himself. Many investigators have ignored this obvious fact, and made the unfortunate attempt to re-shape the whole statue out of bits of fragments which they carefully join together with putty. But they have not noticed that for every broken fragment there is not a

[1] May I note here that recently this problem of the chronological order of the Gospel *pericopes* has been thoroughly investigated by the Giessen Professor, Karl Ludwig Schmidt, *Der Rahmen der Geschichte Jesu* (" The Frame of the History of Jesus ").

suitable fellow, and that parts are lacking between many pieces. The blame for many a wrong track followed by the critics of the Gospel is to be attributed to the use of this mechanical method. In many cases fragments picked up out of this ruinous heap of tradition have been rejected as not belonging because they cannot be made to fit in with other pieces already accepted, whereas it ought to have been recognised that there were pieces missing. This method is also responsible for the artificiality of apologetic : where the pieces did not fit in together, blame was laid on the putty, and lack of this was easily put right. But we cannot reconstruct the whole, the original Jesus, by mechanically putting together the fragments of tradition. The tradition consists, not of a single unitary complex, but of a collection of often isolated single circumstances, short notices about experiences and confessions of Jesus in the most diverse situations. Not seldom the situation is recorded, recorded well ; but often more intimate information is lacking. In every case it is necessary, not to regard the single saying of Jesus as if it were an anonymous, timeless, and lifeless dogmatic sentence, which is to be given its proper place in the system of Jesus, but to reconstruct the situation in which it was spoken or could have been spoken, and out of the confession grasped in this situation, to arrive at the conclusion with regard to the personality of Jesus. The dogmatic method, to use another simile, arranges the single pieces of tradition like pearls on a string, and then supposes that it has in the string of pearls the theological system of Jesus. The historical, psychological method, on the other hand, sees in all the separate words the same single diamond ever sparkling, with ever new blaze, and the glittering stone charms the eye of the observer. The single word of Jesus is not a separate gem, but one of the flashes from the one stone. Behind every word there stands for a moment Jesus Himself. Herein lies the true art of interpreting the words of Jesus. We have to learn to see the detail as characteristic detail, and thus behind and through the word to see His personality. If we use this method of approach, the fragmentary state of the tradition is not nearly so serious a difficulty as it otherwise would be. In many cases we can quickly see at least the main outline and form of the whole.

Things that have been obscured in the original picture of Jesus become clear to one whose eye has become used to looking at the genuine fragments. It was partly the loyalties of popular belief, with its pleasure in the fabulous, that caused these things to be obscured, but also partly the more conscious action of dogmatic and ecclesiastic tendency. Not to speak of obvious and well-known instances, a tendency to alter the original, which we may call weakening the original picture, obtains even to-day amongst the great mass of people who meddle with Jesus in the interest of science or religion. Even to-day, the tendency is overpowering in investigation of the Gospels, preaching, dogma, poetry, and pictorial art, to represent the figure of Jesus as far as possible in the rest of perfect calmness, or if moved, only with the faintest smile of meekness, or with the silent patience of quiet suffering. In very many cases by this means the bounds of the sweetly sentimental are passed. A picture of Jesus emerges which strikes a genuine manly feeling as womanly, a purely womanly feeling as effeminate, and what is even more serious, it is a picture which, to one who knows the tradition, is recognised to be unhistorical.

Even in the oldest tradition, the tendency towards this weakening of the picture is to be seen here and there, but far less than might be expected. This especially is seen in the textual history of certain words of Jesus. But the more we read the words of Jesus with the desire to understand His personality, the more we come upon weightily earnest words of powerful manliness, that lie in the tradition, often like granite blocks in the midst of the splendour of the anemones of the Galilean spring-time. Yes, out of the retirement into which the preference for the easy yoke and the light burden have driven them, words of Jesus spring forth which can only be called heroic.

Our investigation is especially complicated by the fact that in the oldest sources the same detail is sometimes preserved for us in two, three, and even more variations. These variations, which often present questions of the most maddening difficulty for the history of the Gospels and their written and oral sources, are not generally so great a problem for the history of the Gospel and of the characteristics of Jesus, since they are really the business of the textual critic. The experienced investigator would not deem it possible in every case to give preference to a single one of the three evangelists. Even if it appears to him certain that one of the three Gospels is the oldest, he would not make the mistake of valuing the tradition within that oldest Gospel in every case as itself the oldest and most trustworthy; rather, testing each case on its merits, he would give the preference sometimes to this, sometimes to that evangelist; in each case to that one who in the particular case, judged by inner probabilities, deserves credence. This eclectic method is justified in many cases by its own inner logic, but also by the formal character of what is given to us in tradition, which is a vast mosaic made up of many small reminiscences.

This attitude to the sources differs from that of many other scholars. The late Johannes Weiss, of Marburg, later of Heidelberg, once called it " synoptic eclecticism." It is characterised by the fact, already mentioned, that it does not give unvarying preference to any one of the three Synoptic Gospels, declaring that it must be looked upon as the best because the oldest. Such preference is frequently shown. The Gospel of Mark, for instance, is by many considered as the safest foundation of the whole investigation, and in all cases of variation the Marcan tradition is given pre-eminence by those scholars. I too regard the Gospel of

Mark as the oldest of the three Synoptic Gospels, but I do not therefore believe that it is possible to find in every single paragraph of this Gospel the best textual tradition. The sayings of Jesus as preserved by tradition were in the beginning not long chapters, but traditions concerning details, concerning isolated words, or isolated deeds, and they were first transmitted by word of mouth in the Aramaic language; later on they were grouped and written down, also in the Aramaic language; and on the basis of these first groupings our Synoptic Gospels were later built. But even at the time when our Gospels came into existence, oral traditions were still in existence and were used in the composition of our Gospels.

It is therefore necessary to submit every single saying and every single *pericope* (section) to examination by the comparative method, and for such an examination a synopsis is needed. In order to distinguish between primary, secondary and tertiary traditions, we have in the main to follow the principles elaborated by Bentley, Bengel and others to be followed in the textual criticism of the New Testament. I may perhaps here mention a synopsis which was recently published in its sixth edition in Tübingen, by A. Huck. The title of this book, which is equally valuable for students and for those engaged in special research, is *Synopsis of the First Three Gospels*.[1]

What is the significance of John's Gospel for our problem ? These lectures do not afford scope for anything like a full presentation of the great Johannine Problem. But this much must be said : I regard the Gospel of John, and, in still greater measure, the religious attitude which finds its expression in that Gospel and in the other Johannine writings, as a great synthesis of the Synoptic Jesus and the Pauline Christ. John amalgamated ancient, genuine traditions concerning Jesus—traditions which were partly his own recollection—with his experience of com-

[1] *Synopse der drei ersten Evangelien*, J. C. B. Mohr, Tübingen.

munion with Christ, and in this way created a Gospel which was in the first place destined to render service in the worship of the post-Pauline generation, and in the struggle with Gnosticism, Judaism and the followers of John the Baptist. Thus we have in John's Gospel an intimate combination of the tradition concerning Jesus and Christ-mysticism.

I believe that the Jesus-reminiscences, to be found in the Gospel of John, coincide to such a degree with the Synoptic portrait, taken as a whole, that there is no need to emphasise them specially. As an instance let us take the story of the Cleansing of the Temple.[1] Here we find as an utterance of the Johannine Jesus a word which is very characteristic indeed of His communion with God : " Make not my Father's house an house of merchandise." Especially in the original Greek text, this word, in the depth of its meaning, strongly reminds one of the words spoken by the twelve-year-old boy Jesus " Wist ye not that I must be about my Father's business ? " [2]

[1] John 2. 13 ff.   [2] Luke 2. 49.

AND THE FAITH OF PAUL

What I have said will account for the fact that in what I am going to put before you I shall, on the whole, restrict myself to reference to the Synoptic records.

* * *

As regards the method by which we proceed, I have already indicated a good many things which are of importance from the point of view of methodology. Almost everything I have in mind concerning the subject of these lectures has to be ascertained by a method of indirect observation; it cannot be ascertained by any other method. Indirect observation, then, is our method.

It would be possible to apply the method of direct observation if our subject had been the teaching of Jesus. For instance: what does Jesus teach concerning the Law? If it were my task to answer this question, I could rapidly review in my mind a number of direct utterances of Jesus concerning the Law, and rapidly make a summary of His opinions on that basis. But when I wish to study the experiences of Jesus in His communion with God, it is not sufficient to apply the method of direct observation. In the extant records, we find no saying of Jesus on the subject of His communion with God. There was no need for Him to *speak* of communion with God, because He *had* communion with God. It would be in vain to look up the word κοινωνία (communion), as used by Jesus, in a concordance. Even other expressions belonging to this sphere of experience are very rare. There is really only one technical term which I can point to—the Greek word ἐπιγινώσκειν (to know) the Father (Matt. 11. 27).[1] To find this word strikes one as something exceptional, so exceptional that some scholars have referred it to Johannine influence.

Neither do we find any theories about communion with God in the sayings of Jesus, much less do we find the slightest trace of anything like a recommendation of methods

[1] In the parallel passage in Luke 10. 22, the Greek term used is γινώσκειν.

for a mystical sinking of the soul into the divine, or for a gradual raising of the soul from the lower world into the higher—a process which might be represented as culminating in the perfect vision of God. What we do find is a wealth of sayings which, in their totality, point out the one great fact that Jesus *had* communion with God. It is therefore our task to attempt to conceive the traditional sayings of Jesus as reflections of an inward life of intense vitality. That is to say, we must not only try to understand the words themselves, but we must try to look through the words of Jesus into the depths of His soul.

In my opinion, this method of indirect observation is, on the one hand, the only one which makes it possible to understand Jesus, historically and psychologically ; and, on the other hand, it is the best method for the practical preaching of the Gospel in this our time. It is the method which many genuinely inspired preachers of the Gospel have used, sometimes unconsciously. Scientific research concerning Jesus has, I think, a good deal to learn from the method of practical preaching.

In the next lecture we shall attempt to illustrate this method of indirect observation by considering one of the great aspects of the life of Jesus; we shall speak of the prayer life of Jesus as the reflex of His communion with God.

II

THE PRAYER LIFE OF JESUS AS THE REFLEX OF HIS COMMUNION WITH GOD

RELIGION is inner life. To be sure, it brings forth a rich life in history; it inspires and directs the will; it enriches culture; it is consuming fire and vivifying warmth; its volcanic heat leaves the foundation of the centuries trembling. But wherever it has erected monuments or left ruins, there both building and destruction are traceable back to the inner life of certain individual persons. Inner life deals finally with religion; it is a living and moving in God; whether imploring Him or being overwhelmed by Him, whether divining Him or fearing Him, it is always a communion of man with his God.

The position of Jesus in the history of religion is understood when we have understood His inner life. To understand the inner life of Jesus is the chief task of research in early Christianity. What was the communion of Jesus with God? That is the chief question. Many scholars have asked, on the other hand, What did Jesus teach about God? As if the historical position of Jesus was that of a teacher. Jesus did not lecture *de Deo*; He bore witness of God. His teaching of God is a prophetic testimony born out of His inner experience. Jesus preaches about what has been experienced, what has been given, what has been striven for, not what has been brooded over or studied. It is not His system, which one finds in His words, it is His soul. His words and works are self-revealing; when we hear Him speak we listen to the life-throb of His faith and hope, we anticipate the great experiences of life of which He was deemed worthy. His words are not single pieces of an artistic theological mosaic; they are diamond-rays of His personality which shine forth upon us. Of course quite frequently a veil lies over a word of Jesus; we do not know the situation in which it was spoken and so lack something of the personal basis which would permit the dead word to appear as a living testimony. But even in many such cases we can look through the veil to the word and through the word to the depths of His soul. Of course, such an intuitive judgment unavoidably carries with it a subjective element. The most gripping, because the most personal, words of Jesus are undoubtedly those for which the psychological situation has been preserved for us. They permit us to look deep into His personality because we can observe the moment in which they flowed forth from His personality.

Therefore it is not sufficient to ascertain the exact word order and the possible literal meaning of any passage; one must also examine whether or not the passage can be used as a mirror in which the personality of Jesus becomes visible even for a moment. Most of the sayings permit such a procedure. No doubt many even of those which we have been wont to consider anonymous sentences containing some abstract truth, are capable of bringing us into personal contact with the Master ; they permit us to feel His pulse-beat ; they indicate His experiences with modest simplicity. None will leave one with the impression that He is witnessing an ecstasy suggested by an oracle, whose utterances are given forth as imposed wisdom ; but all will more or less clearly establish themselves as testimonies in which Jesus revealed Himself not for the public but for His trusted followers.

Among the most important sources, from which to ascertain the inner life of Jesus, are those which have been delivered to us concerning His prayer-life. In fact, in research in the history of religion the most instructive sources are the prayers and the testimonies about prayer. They characterise a religion, a religious stage, a holy person better than mythology, legend, morality or theosophy. For example, one of the most obvious lacks in the documents of the history

AND THE FAITH OF PAUL 47

of the religion of the Greeks is the fact that comparatively few prayers have been preserved for us. One could write a history of religion as a history of prayer.

In the last few years a great book has been written about prayer, which investigates the whole problem from the broadest religious and historical standpoint, and with the most delicate understanding for the religious psychological problem ; Friedrich Heiler, *Das Gebet : Eine religionsgeschichtliche und religionspsychologische Untersuchung*, 4te Aufl., Munich, 1921.[1] Friedrich Heiler is one of the most interesting figures in present-day theology. He sprang from the Roman Catholic Church, became a Protestant, not without strong influence from Archbishop Söderblom. He is a German Protestant, rather of the Swedish type. He is now professor of theology in Marburg. I might here draw attention to another work of great value for our discussion, by Rudolf Otto, *Das Heilige*, that

[1] *Prayer ; an Investigation in the History and Psychology of Religion.*

has gone through many editions in Germany. I am glad to say that Mr. John W. Harvey of the University of Birmingham has just finished an English translation of this book.[1] Both of the books are among the most valuable that have appeared within the late black years.

But to return to our theme. One comes closest to the soul of the Master when he can listen to the life-throbs of His prayer. Investigations of "the Kingdom of God," "the Son of Man," and other concepts, whatever they be called, deserve all honour. But he who ignores the prayers of Jesus, or passes over them casually with a note, remains standing without the curtain, instead of entering into the Holy of Holies.

* * *

Jesus had a rich prayer-life. A Son of Israel, He had grown up in the atmosphere of the Psalter, of the testimony "Hear, O Israel," and of the deeply experienced, con-

[1] *The Idea of the Holy.* Oxford: Clarendon Press.

AND THE FAITH OF PAUL 49

sccrated praying and thanksgiving which are contained in the older parts of the Schmone Esre-Prayer, the Prayer of the Eighteen Petitions. No piece of bread was broken, no grape was enjoyed without thanks. That prayer among the Jews in Jesus' time had sunk to mere mechanical lip utterances can only be asserted by the advocates of Christianity who believe they honour their Lord by dishonouring His home. In spite of all the public exhibition of the practice of prayer, in spite of the prayer-casuistry of the theologians of Jesus' time, there was as little lack of persons who prayed reverently as among the Catholics at the time of the Reformation. Beside the praying Pharisee stands the praying publican : Jesus Himself pointed out this situation in relating that parable.[1] That He was a child of a praying home and a praying nation requires no proof. Piously He practises the custom of table-prayer.[2] He lives so much in the Psalter that He cries to His God in the words of the

[1] Luke 18. 9 ff.   [2] Matt. 14. 19 ; 15. 36 ; 26. 26.

Psalms when the anguish of death chokes His own words;[1] He designated the commandment beginning "Hear, O Israel"[2] as the most important, as He also bore the symbolic sign prescribed in "Hear, O Israel" on His own garment.[3]

But Jesus did not pray out of inherited piety alone; He spoke with His God not only in the old true forms which are passed on from generation to generation by mothers, but also in a self-sustaining prayer-life, to which the Gospels make frequent reference: "And in the morning, rising up a great while before day, he went out, and departed into a solitary place, and there prayed."[4] "He departed into a mountain to pray."[5] "And it came to pass in those days, that he went out into a mountain to pray, and continued all night in prayer to God."[6] "And it came to pass as he was alone praying . . ."[7] "He took Peter and John and James and

---

[1] Mark 15. 34. [2] Mark 12. 29–30.
[3] See Luke 8. 44. [4] Mark 1. 35. [5] Mark 6. 46.
[6] Luke 6. 12. [7] Luke 9. 18.

went up into a mountain to pray."[1] "And it came to pass that as he was praying in a certain place . . ."[2]

Whoever meets these wonderful short sentences with only a minimum of understanding will know that here lie the roots of the inner life of Jesus. Naturally they do not lie bare and visible before our eyes. With the words to His disciples, "But thou, when thou prayest, enter into thy closet, and when thou hast shut thy door, pray to thy Father which is in secret,"[3] the praying Jesus disclosed Himself; looking through these words, we see Jesus Himself in the night in a lonely desert place bent on His knees; He is alone with His God and what He said to Him is not recorded by the pen of any man. The roots of the cedar are hidden in the holy soil of the earth.

* * *

And yet a few of the strongest roots are open to the daylight for a few spans. That

[1] Luke 9. 28. [2] Luke 11. 1. [3] Matt. 6. 6.

only a few prayers of Jesus have come down to us is a result of the nature of His prayers and speaks well for the trustworthiness of those we have.

Of course, it is to be regretted that we have record of only so few prayers of Jesus ; but we must understand that it could not be otherwise with Him. When we compare the enormous mass of literary prayers which has been produced during the two thousand years of Christianity with the few lines we have from Him, one might naturally be afraid at the poverty of the tradition about Jesus. But no fear is necessary. These few lines outbalance the whole mass of literary prayers.

Anyone who ventures to study prayer literature, the books of prayers for private use, and the liturgies of churches, will find that the true spirit of prayer is absent from a large part of these texts. The simplicity of prayer is absent from them. It is actors, not praying men, who stand or sit before us. In the case of many a liturgical prayer, one must conclude that the author has sat

AND THE FAITH OF PAUL 53

himself down to compose a prayer. One hears the noise of the machine into which the prayer has been dictated. The very worst are the ones that have been specially manufactured by the group work of commissions, where the morning bloom of eternity has been brushed off by the interfering finger of the expert in prayer and where one notices instead of the primitive growth of true prayer, the artificial compromise of literary stylists.

Jesus never sat Himself down to make a prayer. The Lord's Prayer itself was not produced like the liturgical prayers of a commission that is composing a prayer-book. And so we dare to say that, though there are only very few lines that we possess about the prayer life of Jesus, these few are testimonies of genuine prayer, and it is especially in connection with these that the task which is indicated in the first lecture can most easily be carried out. In fact those short prayers in Gethsemane and from the Cross have never grown cold, and their original fire will never pass away.

54 THE RELIGION OF JESUS

That these prayers which have come down to us are unusually short is a proof of their genuineness. There could have been only a few entirely exceptional instances in which the disciples could have listened to the praying Jesus. But what they realised in such breathless moments they could never forget. Indeed, as the words of Jesus were translated for Greek disciples, when it came to His prayers, here and there even the original Semitic word-order was not recast into Greek, and the "Abba" of the praying Jesus [1] resounded as far as Galatia [2] and Rome [3] and is found to-day in all the languages into which the Bible is translated.

Jesus Himself once pointed out the content of one of His prayers: "Simon, Simon, behold Satan hath desired to have you, that he may sift you as wheat: but I have prayed for thee that thy faith fail not." [4] Here is the intercessory prayer of Jesus, interceding for His disciple, for an undying

---

[1] Mark 14. 36.
[2] Gal. 4. 6.
[3] Rom. 8. 15.
[4] Luke 22. 31, 32.

AND THE FAITH OF PAUL 55

human soul which must be saved from the enticing onslaughts of Satan. Jesus knows His disciple; both a follower and a Satan can be found in Peter. The same experience which prompted the Master to say at one time to Peter, " Get thee behind me, Satan: for thou savourest not the things that be of God, but the things that be of men,"[1] now permits Him to pray for the disciple. Face to face with Peter, holy indignation and flaming denunciation! Face to face with the Father, interceding mercy!

Two other prayers which have come down to us verbally, the prayer of praise and the prayer at Gethsemane, can be designated the polar extremes of the prayer attitude of Jesus.

The prayer of praise has been preserved by both Matthew and Luke. The latter gives us also the unique situation which elicited it. It came from the Master's lips when the disciples, who had been sent out by Him, returned rejoicing about their victories over demons. At that time Jesus said to them:

[1] Mark 8. 29, 33.

"Rejoice not that the spirits are subject unto you; but rather rejoice, because your names are written in heaven."[1] "In that same hour," Luke continues, "He rejoiced in the spirit and said: I thank thee, O Father, Lord of heaven and earth, that thou hast hid these things from the wise and prudent and hast revealed them unto babes: even so, Father; for so it seemed good in thy sight."[2]

Luke's preservation of the facts which led up to this prayer is one of the many jewels which he has added to our knowledge of the life of Jesus. Only through the situation do we clearly understand the prayer. It is a shout of joy, a shout of exultation, a shout of rejoicing. Jesus is standing upon a Tabor of His inner life; to the small group of His humble, despised, and unlearned disciples, something great and unspeakably powerful has been granted. Even the reason of the learned and wise does not possess what they

[1] Luke 10. 20.
[2] Luke 10. 21; see also Matt. 11. 25, 26.

AND THE FAITH OF PAUL

possess, what has been revealed to them. " Blessed are the poor in spirit, for theirs is the Kingdom of Heaven!" But this is not His triumph; it is the Father's doing; to Him it has been well-pleasing. The Ruler of heaven and earth has revealed Himself to the humble. This is the certainty which fills the breast of Jesus and raises the shout of exultation to His lips. The Son stands before the Father, the humble before the Lord, full of unspeakable joy, the whole soul a thank-offering to the living God.

The prayer of Gethsemane leads us from this height to the darkest depths. Mark has given us the best account: " And he said, Abba, Father, all things are possible unto thee; take away this cup from me: nevertheless not what I will, but what thou wilt." [1] Three times Jesus repeated this prayer; the inner condition He Himself described to His disciples: " My soul is exceeding sorrowful unto death." [2]

The Evangelist relates in this connection

[1] Mark 14. 36.   [2] Mark 14. 34.

that Jesus had begun to tremble and be sorely troubled.[1] Luke [2] reports that drops of perspiration became as drops of blood, and an early Christian writer, mentioning the Passion,[3] is deeply moved by the loud cries and the tears of the praying one. Jesus sees Himself in the hands of His mortal enemies; He foresees His martyrdom; He anticipates the worst; His soul trembles with real feeling, unrelieved by an unnatural stoicism. With the healthy person's natural shrinking from death, He sinks upon His knees before the Father, and raises to Him, once, twice, and even a third time, an appeal for help so poignant and yet so simple, that the gods of Oedipus and the God of Job never received one like it, a petition and at the same time a submission. There is no indication that He was obstinate or egoistic. The "I" is placed under the "Thy"— "Not what I will, but thy will be done."[4]

[1] Mark 14. 33. [2] Luke 22. 44. [3] Heb. 5. 7.

[4] The question of the genuineness of the prayer in Gethsemane is naturally of great importance. Against the genuineness, it has been maintained that according to the tradition of the three Synoptics, the disciples

The importance of the three prayer-sayings of the Crucified on Golgotha can scarcely be measured. They are an intercession, a cry of despair, and a groan of completion. While He was being nailed to the cross, or just after that, Jesus prayed : " Father, forgive them ; they know not what they do." [1] This fact of intercession shows that Jesus' command to love and pray for our enemies [2] is amongst those words which cannot be separated from His personality without taking away the best part of their meaning. It is uncritical to doubt the genuineness of the

---

were asleep, and so could not know what Jesus prayed. I believe this to be a mistaken criticism. The content of the prayer in Gethsemane fits so badly into a dogmatic conception of Christ, that we can scarcely assume that in the later times of the Christ-cult it was first ascribed to Jesus. There seems to be a strong inner argument for its genuineness. I believe it is not the prayer that is a secondary feature of the story, but the sleeping disciples. That detail has probably arisen through a misunderstanding of the word of Jesus : " Watch and pray, that ye enter not into temptation." It has been assumed that the command " Watch," was to be taken literally, and the conclusion was drawn from it, that the disciples had already slept.

[1] Luke 23. 34.   [2] Luke 6. 28 ; cf. Matt. 5. 44.

prayer upon the cross because it might have been placed in His mouth as an illustration of His command. As if it were child's play to utter such a command, and as if Jesus could have commanded the prayer of intercession for His enemies without Himself practising the intercession. This example of the cross is only one of many similar instances; we can surmise that Jesus in His regular nightly prayers was frequently concerned for those on whom the prophetic warnings of coming wrath had exerted no influence. The commandment is not the presupposition of this intercession but its fruit. There is no valid reason for doubting the tradition that Luke has given us. What a deep insight into the soul of Jesus is given by this prayer for His executioners! What trust the crucified Son of Israel has in His God! Where is the Psalmist's God of vengeance? Where is the God of the Maccabean martyrs, who was receptive both of faith and hate?

Still less can one doubt the genuineness of the Crucified's piercing cry of need. It cannot be fitted into any dogmatically developed presentation of Jesus. Why should it have been placed in His mouth? It agrees only with the real cross. "With a loud voice" the dying Jesus cried out, and His original Aramaic words resound down eighteen centuries: " Elói, Elói, lama sebachthani? " which is, being interpreted: "My God, my God, why hast Thou forsaken me?"[1] Jesus did not create the words of this prayer, but they were none the less His possession bought by His life's blood. In like manner, ages before, a human soul in deep need had thirsted after the living God in the twenty-second Psalm. Now these words are found on the parched lips of Jesus. They cannot be classified under the usual categories of

[1] Mark 15. 34; Matt. 27. 46. The tradition of this prayer is, as is well known, varied in the manuscripts. Both an Aramaic and a Hebrew form of the words have come down to us. It is more than probable that Jesus prayed in Aramaic, and that the Hebrew form has arisen in later times through assimilation to the Hebrew Old Testament. Perhaps I should mention that, as Wellhausen has pointed out, one ought to pronounce the Elói with emphasis on the o.

prayer; they are not even a petition, but the groan of a martyr, and still a prayer as genuine as any other. This prayer with its whole elementary burden of need accomplishes more than a hundred comfortable theses against the reasonableness of prayer. This prayer teaches prayer, and it teaches everyone whose faith is a sure inherited wisdom, disturbed by nothing, that communion with God signifies a struggle for God, a struggle between God-nearness and God-forsakenness.

Jesus emerged victor. His words of victory, again " with a loud voice," are the prayer: " Father, into thy hands I commend my spirit." [1]

These words of the dying Jesus are also a prayer of old time; with the exception of the first word it comes from the thirty-first Psalm; but it is also the personal possession of the praying Saviour on the cross; Jesus added only a single word to the words of the Psalmist, a word understood in its full richness only when it is conceived as a word of

[1] Luke 23. 46.

prayer—" Abba," " Father." With this loudly on his lips Jesus " gave up the ghost."

* * *

As if face to face we can see the praying One in His own prayers. In the words to His disciples which deal with prayer we see Him again as in a mirror. Here the method of indirect observation, which I mentioned in the first lecture, is in place. One must not assume that Jesus gave these words about prayer to His disciples merely as cold maxims. Rather a clear reflection of His own prayer life is to be seen in them. We have already noticed that the command to pray for one's enemies indicated the content of His own intercession. Likewise it is also with the admonition to pray for workers in God's harvest.[1]

Above all we see the praying Jesus in the Lord's Prayer. To be sure, it is a prayer for His disciples to pray, but Jesus here also has given His best, the ripe fruits of His own prayer-experience. It is a bad exposition

[1] Matt. 9. 35–38.

to deprive the Lord's Prayer of personal contact with the Lord, just as it is dogmatic affectation to make a deep chasm between "my Father" and "our Father" in the words of Jesus. The Lord's Prayer was not given by Jesus as the foundation stone of an impersonal liturgy for a new cult; on the contrary, Jesus as a praying Master taught His followers to pray through this example of prayer. We gain from it a conception of the modest earnestness and humble power of His own praying.

Even where Jesus criticises the prayer-practices of those holy only in appearance and of the heathen [1] He reveals the type of His own praying. Only hypocrites pray on street-corners; He prays in His "inner chamber." The heathen and the Pharisees [2] babble liturgies filled with rich words; His prayers are short; for a son prays to His Father, and the Father knows what the child needs even before he asks.

This last thought is unique and highly significant; God does not need our prayers.

[1] Matt. 6. 5 ff. [2] Mark 12. 40; cf. Matt. 23. 14.

AND THE FAITH OF PAUL

This is a warning, not against the prayer of petition, but against the unchildlike stubborn prayer, against the prayer of petition that is thought of as compelling magic. How energetically Jesus practised the true prayer of petition needs no long proof; out of the secrecy of His personal petitions and supplications the wonderful parables of the petitioning friend,[1] the petitioning child,[2] and the petitioning widow [3] were uttered.

The simplicity of His prayers was undisturbed by any shadow of doctrinal reflection. Mountain-moving faith permits Him to ask; therefore He can testify: " Have faith in God. For verily I say unto you, That whosoever shall say unto this mountain, Be thou removed, and be thou cast into the sea; and shall not doubt in his heart, but shall believe that those things which he saith shall come to pass; he shall have whatsoever he saith. Therefore I say unto you, What things soever ye desire, when ye pray, believe that ye receive them, and ye shall have them." [4]

[1] Luke 11. 5-8. [2] Luke 11. 11-13; cf. Matt. 7. 9-11.
[3] Luke 18. 1-8. [4] Mark 11. 22-24; cf. Matt. 17. 20.

This is one of the most certainly genuine of the words of Jesus (even Paul uses it) ; [1] it bears witness to the wonderful paradox of the power of prayer which is effective beyond all understanding. Likewise the kindred passage : " If ye had faith as a grain of mustard seed, ye might say unto this sycamine tree, Be thou plucked up by the root, and be thou planted in the sea ; and it should obey you." [2] Jesus probably plays on this word also in Matthew 21. 21 ; Matthew refers it, of course, to the previously related story of the withered fig-tree.[3]

One cannot weaken anything here even if the paradox in the form of the words cannot at once be explained. The one who prays in faith has miraculous power. This is what Jesus wishes to say ; and that He asserts nothing other than His own prayer-experience can be clearly deduced from the splendidly reported story of the healing of the deaf-mute.[4]

[1] 1 Cor. 13. 2. [2] Luke 17. 6.

[3] For a fuller treatment of this passage see appendix to Chapter III. *The Fig Tree*, p. 98.

[4] Mark 7. 34 ; cf. Mark 6. 41 ; 9. 29 ; and Matt. 26. 53.

AND THE FAITH OF PAUL 67

A look toward heaven, and a sighing prayer goes up with the mighty Ephphatha.

* * *

In prayer Jesus communes with His God. The child speaks with the Father. His prayer can be both a quiet petition or a passionate supplication, a shout of joy or a cry of pain. At one time the heavens open over the praying One; at another a dark cloud seems to obtrude itself between the Son and His Father. But the Father hears each prayer; for the praying One does not desire to gain by His " much speaking." The Father's will shall be done. And if the praying One could gain everything with His believing prayer, still in His great hour of passion He does not ask for twelve legions of angels. He does pray that the cup may pass, but He annuls this petition: " Not my will, but thine be done." In the prayer self retires; Jesus prays for God's harvest and God's kingdom, for the endangered disciples, for the silent and lowly brother. And the grace given to the humble causes Him to shout forth in words of thanks. Prayer is for Him a holy matter, so holy that the world is not permitted to witness it, and so serious that too much is evil. Prayer is something self-understood and still not necessary for God; something wonderfully powerful and yet not a magical remedy.

The question, In what relation was Jesus to His God? is largely one with the question, How did Jesus pray? Father and Lord—so Jesus in praise called the Eternal; this is more than an inherited form for Him; it is the testimony of His own inner experience of God. All that is given to us of His idea of God, the whole Gospel, refers back to this final experience. In experiencing God as the Father Jesus experiences the mercy and the friendliness, the whole comfort of the living God; in experiencing God as Lord, He experiences the majesty and holiness, the whole earnestness of the living God. Upon the countenance of the praying Jesus rests the clear reflection of the countenance of His God.

III

THE COMMUNION OF JESUS WITH GOD THE FATHER AND GOD THE LORD

THE central question for the history of religion, and for religion in general, is, " What communion had Jesus with God ? " It is to a large extent the same with the question, " How did Jesus pray ? " " Father " and " Lord "—that is how Jesus experienced His God in prayer. " Father " and " Lord " are with Him more than merely traditional formulæ. They are the shortest confessions of His experience of God. All that has come down by tradition to us of His sayings is contained in this twofold experience, which yet is one. If it were only the teaching of Jesus about God with which we were concerned, we should not on this point find anything absolutely original. Both names of God, " Father " and " Lord " are old Jewish.

Jesus here again shows to us His unity of soul with His religious homeland.

Therefore our first task is to gain a picture of the relation between the spiritual life of Jesus, and that of His own people. Here there are two sets of facts to be observed. First, His general relation with His home, and then His especial relationship with John the Baptist.

* * *

Between the Old and the New, there is nowhere an unbridgeable gulf. Those who hope to separate the Gospel entirely from the Old Testament and from Judaism are cutting the vine away from its roots. "*Novum Testamentum in Vetere latet*"—" The New Testament lies hidden in the Old." Jesus is so great that He can dispense with the efforts of those who seek to glorify Him at the expense of His ancestors.

His ancestors had preserved a great possession even through the time when the Roman oppression was at its severest. Certainly the revelation of the Eternal (praised be His name) lay hid in the treasure-chamber of the Holy Scriptures. The revelation was out of the great past, but it was at the same time the revelation for all the future of the will of God, the Law and the Prophets. It was read and heard in the Sabbath congregation of the worshippers, spelt out by the children who learnt the Aleph, Beth and Gimel from it, explained by theologians, lawyers and pious thinkers, by the grey-headed before whose gentle and delicate wisdom we stand respectfully, and by advocates of the letter whose artificiality leaves us cold, but by all, with the defiant prancing passion of the politically oppressed, it was treasured as the best of all goods. As the national property, the Bible of the Old Testament gives to Jewish piety in the period of Roman oppression its characteristic feature.

This we see on two sides. As it was itself a document, not only of prophetic faith, but also of faithfulness to the Law, and thus wears two faces, so it influenced the religious history of Judaism in two directions, both impeding and forwarding, both enslaving and freeing, and by that means brought to birth the future fate of a historical religious conflict for Judaism. It was leading-strings for the one party; it lent wings to the other.

To those for whom the Old Testament was leading-strings, religion was law, a walking according to the definitely prescribed line of tradition. Such religion was essentially facing towards the past. Revelation lay in the past, and the duty of the present was continually to decipher afresh the hieroglyphics of an earlier age. After the decipherers came the interpreters of the decipherers, and the next generations wrote the commentaries on the interpreters of the decipherers of the Scriptures. So was formed, so grew in power, the class of the scribes. Theology came to the front, authorities allowed approach to authority, casuistry threw its net out, every single person became a member of the whole led mass, prayer became a formula, the service of God became divine service.

The same Bible which married piety to the dogmatic legal book religion, that is to say, to the past, also had the power to bring men into contact with free Grace, and make them behold a future destined for them by the living God. From the prophets and from the Psalms, as also from the prophetic sayings of the Law, there streamed forth to men's minds an unconquerable living knowledge of God.

But contact with prophets is, at second hand, contact with God Himself. It was possible for many to experience a rising up with wings like eagles, and this was more strongly experienced, the more miserable was their present lot. By those who had complete possession of prophetic confidence in God, mere legality was felt either as an enemy, or as something that had passed out of the view of the eye that was intoxicated with light ; or, again, its commands were simply observed as a pious usage. But in every case, prophetic confidence separated itself clearly from legality. Its gaze was not directed to the past so much as to the future. It did not remain a dogmatic faith in times gone by, but an inspired belief in the present, and even more in the future. The best is yet to be, the golden age lies before us. For the living God, who in the past ages did signs and wonders as Creator of the world, and as Shepherd of His people, He Himself will yet bring about the greatest thing of all ; He will call into being the new Heaven and the new Earth, and then will come Redemption for His people. In experience and confession which were near akin to the vision and the speech of the poet, this prophetic confidence worked out in enthusiasm, in wrestling in prayer, in revelation and in psalm.

This confidence which burned and worked in Jewish religion under the apparently quiet surface of legality, and which finds its summit in the expectation of a God-anointed Redeemer, an Anointed One who is to bring about the Kingdom of God—this we call the Messianic hope. Not Messianic dogmatic or apocalyptic — these mere names are not adequate for such blazing confidence, because they have made a doctrinaire petrification of what was movement and growth. Certainly the Messianic hope did not lack primitive traditions and its literature did not lack traditional ornament—horns, trumpets, seals, and so forth—but it is triviality to attempt to bring into a system of paragraphs and chapters all the individual items of popular longing and hoping that are to be found in documents recording three hundred years of Messianic expectation.

We are not concerned here with a closely knit body of thought worked out and built up from the quiet speculation of the schools, but with impressionist pictures of the future, rich and joyful in colour, mostly related to one another in style, by unknown masters of popular art, whose meaning is to be grasped by a single glance without long searching. All these pictures say, in antique oriental Jewish colours, not seldom with exaggerations into the grotesque, miraculous, fantastic and horrible, what the most genuine of genuine piety is: they testify the certainty that God is present, God is active, God helps, God rescues, God redeems.

This certainty has, along with it, a strong dash of Zionist patriotism: help, rescue, redemption, are expected from God's Anointed, and His Kingdom is expected for the enslaved people of God. The tone of these hopes for the future can be very different: soft longings as of a bride here, defiant shaking of the iron bars of the dungeon there; it paints for the one psalms of peace before his soul, and puts the harp in his hand: for the other, it sharpens the Maccabean sword and speaks to him of the thunder of the judgment.

Jewish religion of the latest period is, through the Bible, a power that works in different ways, some above, some below, and some mingled with each other. Born and brought up in the leading-strings of the *Thora*, Legality gives to Judaism, in the first place to its upper stratum, a peculiar hardness, doctrinaire completeness and de-

AND THE FAITH OF PAUL 77

pendence upon the past. It is prophesying about divine learning and church law, about a parchment library of volumes. Begotten and given wings by the prophets, the Messianic Hope lent to Judaism, especially to its middle and lower strata, peculiar strength, immediacy, freshness, and forward-looking boldness. It gave to the Jew his lost self again, his religion and his strength for the conflict. Its prophecy was of God and His Kingdom, of men, prophets, martyrs: Elijah was to come again, and after him on the way prepared for him, the Lord's Anointed Himself.

* * *

And Elijah came. In the fifteenth year of the Emperor Tiberius there was a rumour in Jerusalem of the appearance of John, a son of the Priests. In the wilderness of Judæa the masses streamed to him and listened to his mighty commission: The Kingdom, he said, was near! Under the influence of the power of this Message, people accepted the command : Change your minds ! Mass revivals took place, innumerable people confessed their sins and had their guilt washed away in Jordan by John. The whole country was in movement. Strange tales were told of the outward appearance of the man ; serious, cutting, sharp words of the Baptist flew from mouth to mouth, testimonies of the Messiah and of the Judgment. The prince of the country feared political unrest ; he had the daring man, whose call to repentance had penetrated even into the ladies' bower of his palace, taken prisoner and imprisoned in the castle of Machærus on the East of the Dead Sea. There, after a long imprisonment, John fell the victim to the revenge of a devilish woman.

What we know of him is not much. It is only the shadow of the Baptist that falls on the great stage of the Gospel History, but it is truly a great shadow. One or two expressions of opinion by Jesus let us gather more about the Baptist than the occasional remarks of the evangelists, or of the historian

Josephus. We see thereby what this man in fact meant for his people or for Jesus Himself. Naturally the figure of the ascetic deeply impressed itself upon the popular tradition, his camel's-hair garment, his leathern girdle, his scanty fare, all the desert could afford. Jesus also spoke of him as an ascetic, and the narrower circle of John's disciples honoured ascetic practice.

But most popularly he was the Baptist. So Jesus and his contemporaries already called him. The symbolism of the Baptism of John was at once obvious to every Oriental mind, but especially so to the Jew, who alongside his ritual washings was acquainted with the baptism of the Proselyte on his conversion to the law: to the one it meant what to the other it was, the washing away of the old man. John himself had warned against an overvaluation of his Baptism: the real Baptism was to be brought by the Coming One who would be stronger than he; He would baptise with Spirit and fire.

For all this the exact position of the Baptist

in the history of Religion is not yet fully known. Again it is Jesus whose verdict illuminates for a moment like lightning his personality otherwise shrouded in darkness: Jesus had the impression of John that he must be the Elijah who was to come again, —that he was a prophet, yes, that he was more than a prophet, the greatest of those born of woman.[1] It is through this verdict of a contemporary, a verdict which was also that of an eyewitness and of one who knew mankind, that John receives his position in history. John stands along with Isaiah and Jeremiah, the giant figures of the Semitic East.

He had nourished his soul on the great prophets of the past and from them had learnt to speak. The few sentences which we have of his are full of the marrow of prophecy. Prophetic was his whole attitude, prophetic his taking the part of those who have no coat and no bread, prophetic his ruthless opposition to the infatuated rulers. He was prophetic as a man of the people, as

[1] Matt. 11. 9–11; cf. Luke 7. 26–28.

a preacher of repentance and as herald of the Messiah. As he stood there before the masses—Jesus once sketched for us his portrait—altogether earnest, proud, unbending, true to himself, rude and harsh without any monkish burlesque about him! " God wills it " ; with this in their minds the very masses, who were most deeply affected by him in their national pride, thronged, filled with inner contrition from his preaching, to his Baptism, and even those who rejected him could not but call him demonic.

The essential content of his preaching to the people was the demand for a renewing of the mind on account of the coming Kingdom. Inwardness instead of the striving for outward advantages, humanity as a proof of piety, that was " the way of Righteousness " which this prophet showed. And no time was to be lost : the axe was already laid to the root of the trees, and already the mightier stood ready with his fan, to cleanse the threshing-floor. John thought of the coming Kingdom as a state, which, after the judgment by the Messiah, was to come about, without doubt, here on earth. He who denies this fact, in order to relieve the Baptist of a this-worldly hope, does not know that he thereby takes away the best of his message, the prophetic humanity in the power of which he had confidence in God and in His Anointed that they had the power to transform even this evil world. It is for this reason that his ideal of the Kingdom has no millennial features, but is ethical through and through. The coming Kingdom is a Kingdom of purified, earnest, inward, merciful men.

Between Jesus of Nazareth and John the Baptist there must have been some very intimate personal connection. From the words of Jesus about John the Baptist we can see indirectly that it was not simply that Jesus had an intimate acquaintance with John the Baptist as a prophet, but that it was through the powerful impression which the greatness of the Baptist and his divine mission had upon Him, that He Himself was forced into His public mission. It is the importance of the Baptist for Jesus, and thereby his importance for the history of religion, that he not only predisposed the masses to receive the Gospel, but that he also in the personality of Jesus set free prophetic power which lay hidden there.

His general religious attitude Jesus had inherited from His ancestors; the normal, quiet piety which, like the gentle sunshine, lighted and warmed His whole being. Everything else of prophecy and expectation of the Kingdom of God was set in vibration in Him through His contact with the Baptist. Where we see the summer lightning of the Messianic presentiment and confession, the history of religion points us each time to contact with the Baptist. Of this second feature we hope to speak in the last two lectures. To-day we must speak of the first, of the natural breathing of His religious inner life.

A great symbol of the spiritual fellowship of Jesus with His religious home is the history of the twelve-year-old Jesus in the Temple.[1] I hold it to be not only a symbol, but, on account of its entire simplicity, a true tradition. Exegetes ought not to make it artificially difficult. Of most of the great religious figures of the past, there have been stories of their childhood told, which are more or less influenced by ideas derived from the cult they have founded, especially from the idea that the Saint even as a child had done great miracles. The tradition about Jesus Himself in later times, as is well known, showed developments of this kind. In the apocryphal gospels we find numerous stories of the miraculous deeds of the child Jesus. How absolutely different is this story! At no point does it go beyond what is childlike. I mean " childlike " not in the average sense. There is the child who is gifted of God, a peculiarly gifted child, yet for all that a genuine child. No miracle-worker in the garb of a boy.

Already here, in this single tradition about

[1] Luke 2. 41–52.

AND THE FAITH OF PAUL 85

His youth, it is to be noticed that He calls God His father.[1] " My Father." It is not meant dogmatically, in an exclusive sense, as if Jesus intended to say " He is not *your* Father " ; but it is spoken from simple experience. The man, Jesus, uses exactly the same expression, when He says : " Make not my Father's house a house of merchandise." [2] This is one of the passages in John's Gospel which depends upon old, primary tradition.

And thus must one read all that stands in the tradition of His own confessions and of words to His disciples, which spring out of His own experience. One ought not to look at the surface only with the curious question : What is there new in this teaching, in relation to the Psalter, to Philo or to Seneca ?—but, looking into the depths of such expressions, we should see through them the heat and glow of the hour of their first utterance.

In the experience of communion with the Father, Jesus learnt the mercy and friendli-

[1] Luke 2. 49.   [2] John 2. 16.

ness, the whole comfort of the living God. Not that He invented the name " Father." In the whole realm of the religious civilisation of the Mediterranean world there was nothing unusual for a people to call God, or a god, " Father." In the Old Testament, in Jewish religion, as well as in Græco-Roman antiquity and elsewhere, it is common enough. So Jesus when He prays " Abba " in Gethsemane shows the influence of His mother's prayer.

The name " Father " is an old gold coin. But where else did it bear the impress that Jesus gave it?

Jesus had so experienced the mystery of divine sonship that He, in a moment of overflowing thankfulness, could confess that everything was delivered to Him of His Father; that no man knew the Father but the Son, and he to whom the Son willed to reveal Him, and that no man knew the Son but the Father. He thus claimed the whole knowledge of what the Father is, and with it the complete possession of the grace that comes to him who knows God. The unbounded truth of this claim might be doubted, if the content of His knowledge of God had been something complicated, but the greatness, the divine simplicity of its content, is the seal of its genuineness.

There are at bottom two closely related elements of consciousness which are portrayed in His confessions of the Father. God is the faithfulness that cares for men, and the grace that forgives. Numerous words of comfort bear witness to the providential love of God, which can be depended upon for the very smallest of all His creation, from the anemones of the field, and the sparrow and raven, right up to mankind, both good and bad. These words of Jesus are never mechanical and literal prescriptions for special circumstances, but directing posts for the spirit, often touched with the conscious, smiling paradox of casuistic exaggeration.

Their background of Oriental civilisation must not be overlooked. It sounds a paradox, yet there is something true in the statement, that the words of Jesus need to be understood in the atmosphere of their own climate. Through a peculiar experience, I learnt much on this point. About twenty years ago, I gave a course of lectures before a body of working-men in Mannheim on " The Origin of the New Testament." There I cited the words of the Sermon on the Mount : " Behold the fowls of the air, for they sow not, neither do they reap nor gather into barns, yet your Heavenly Father feedeth them." [1] In the question box I found afterwards an objection, which though it was written in unpractised hand, and with many mistakes, impressed me deeply. " It is not true that God cares for the birds. In a cold winter they freeze by thousands." The man felt quite rightly, viewing it from the standpoint of our northern, western land. By the Sea of Genesaret, where these words were spoken, no bird was ever frozen. The climate there is very nearly sub-tropical. In the

[1] Matt. 6. 26.

same way, the words of Jesus on the sending out of the apostles cannot be taken literally as applying to the sending out of missionaries to, say, Greenland or Thibet. The sayings of Jesus cannot be mechanically and literally transplanted into another civilisation. It is for us to transfer the words of Jesus into our climate, our circumstances and our times, and then understand them, not like a code of law, but according to their spirit.

The certainty that even the unrighteous and evil share God's sun and God's rain of itself indicates the connection with the other certainty, that the Father is Grace that forgives sin. The statement that Jesus made the forgiveness of sins, which He preached, secretly dependent upon His own future death, is to be placed among the most poverty-stricken of theological foundlings. He announced the full amnesty of the Father without bargaining and haggling : " Thy sins are forgiven thee." This not indeed to the whole of mankind, or to all then and there present without condition, but to particular people whose inner condition He understood. And He pointed out to everyone, through the ever classical type of the publican smiting his breast, and the Prodigal Son, what was the human and what was the divine part in forgiveness of sins ; mercy on this side, repentance on that. But the mercy of God is never weakly or morally indifferent. As Paul formulated it later, so it was also in the Gospel of Jesus, " the kindness of God leadeth thee to repentance " (that is, to a change of mind).[1] Jesus had a deep conviction of the moral sublimity of His God. He had experienced the Father as Lord.

* * *

" Lord " also is a primitive Semitic name of God, which in the time of Jesus had passed over also into the religions of Western civilisation. But for Jesus it was more than a name, from His mouth the word quivers through us with a suggestion of the limitless, the majestic, the everlasting, the eternal :

[1] Rom. 2. 4.

AND THE FAITH OF PAUL 91

He rules in holiness and righteousness, Who alone is good, a Judge and Destroyer of the evil. He who blasphemes Him, commits the greatest sin. So horrible to Jesus did this sin against the Holy Ghost appear that He declared it to be unforgivable.

Both motives of the consciousness of God are reflected in the inner religious attitude of Jesus. Before the Father He stands as Son with love, trust, joy; before the Lord He bows Himself as the humble slave: " Thy will be done." Yes, Jesus demanded fear, fear before Him who is able to destroy both soul and body in hell.[1]

Now from this experience of God which Jesus had, with its union of severe and gentle, we can understand the position which He held towards sin. And in this also He had no easy and prepared formula; rather, we see contrasts, which when they are hardened into doctrine, become paralysed, but which as the driving powers of a personal life have for ever impressed upon the figure of Jesus

[1] Matt. 10. 28.

the stamp of a Redeemer whose work goes far beyond the bounds of merely national hope. As one who knew human sins right into their most intimate depths and their smallest branchings, Jesus showed in judging them a splendid seriousness,—the reflex of His experience of God as the holy, only good and majestic Lord. Where the self-righteous claims with proud words that he has done good, and left evil undone, there Jesus remorselessly uncovers the spiritual flaws, the lustful thought, the envious eye, the arrogant gesture. The angry word brings us into the same guilt as the hand stained with the murder of a brother. Jesus lays the idea of guilt like a great weight upon the conscience. That we get rid of our guilt, and do not get entangled in new guilt, is for Him just as important as security in daily bread. Other things we need scarcely to pray for ourselves.

The severe judge of sin shows, on the other hand, in dealing with sinners a truly divine gentleness—the reflex of the trust of Jesus in the mercy of God. We can view what the sinner has done as simply the mistake of one who did not know. Where condemnation would appear to be in place, there He can announce forgiveness, and with His whole pure personality He stands the Protector of slandered sinners from the hypocrisy of those who are satisfied with their appearance of holiness. Scarcely anything made Him so indignant as the lack of love towards the fallen, and scarcely anything made Him so joyful as the conversion of a single sinner. Heaven is stirred with joy on its account. That the sinner can be converted is for Him just as sure as the conviction that the sinner ought to be converted. The problem of the freedom of the will is altogether strange to Him. No doctrinaire doubt gnaws at His powerful moral optimism.

* * *

We may gather up all that we have been able to say of the communion of Jesus with God as Father and as Lord, something as follows :—

The communion of Jesus with God is a fellowship of Love with the Father, and a fellowship of Will with the Lord. And both can be included in one powerful fundamental word: πίστις, "faith." In the words of Jesus there is not much said about faith and belief, but we have a few words which make it clear to us that for Jesus faith was something quite extraordinary. These are the words which I have already quoted to you in speaking of the Fig Tree: "If ye had faith as a grain of mustard seed, ye might say unto this sycamine tree, Be thou plucked up by the root, and be thou planted in the sea, and it should obey you;"[1] and again: "If ye have faith, and doubt not, ye shall not only do that about the fig tree, but also if ye shall say unto this mountain, Be thou removed and be thou cast into the sea, it shall be done."[2] In these words, the following is obviously implied: faith in the experience of Jesus is trust in the living God, and this trust represents a dynamic contact between God and the believer. This is seen especially when the believer prays: "And

[1] Luke 17. 6.   [2] Matt. 21. 21.

all things whatsoever ye shall ask in prayer believing, ye shall receive." [1] Compare also: " If thou canst believe: all things are possible to him that believeth." [2]

This is a quite peculiar conception of faith, a *fides heroica et mirifica*—" a heroic and miraculous faith." One ought not to destroy the paradoxical greatness of this conception by Philistine exegesis. It is the faith of Jesus, it is His own faith that Jesus here implies. We should guard ourselves against the temerity of thinking that we are able to copy Jesus. The following of Jesus consists less in attempting to imitate His experiences, than in submitting oneself to Him. With us the word " faith " is one of the most commonly used, and one whose meaning has become most attenuated. An enormous mass of literature on the nature of faith has very nearly smothered faith itself. In those words about the faith that can move mountains, Jesus stands before us absolutely without literature and paper, but as one who believes ;

[1] Matt. 21. 22.   [2] Mark 9. 23.

and there are scarcely any other words of Jesus that still show so clearly the volcanic fire of their first utterance as these words. Yes, truly the faith of Jesus in God His Father and His Lord is like a volcano. Our faith is like a flickering candle.

There is one passage in the Gospels which shows the overwhelming power of the faith of Jesus upon another believer.

Jesus spoke that word to the father of the dumb and deaf demoniac boy: " If thou canst believe ; all things are possible to him that believeth." Thereupon the father of the child said the words : " Lord, I believe ; help thou mine unbelief." [1] If Mark had only passed on to us this single phrase, he would have done us an immense service thereby. These words are among the most remarkable words of mankind. They are most full of meaning, and most important. " I believe ; help thou mine unbelief "—that is the confession of the believing man. He is a believer when he puts himself under the

[1] Mark 9. 24.

influence of the powerful, believing personality of Jesus. He feels himself unbelieving when he dares to compare himself with Him. This one picture—the believing Jesus, and the believing-unbelieving man—perhaps gives us the deepest insight into the communion of Jesus with God.

APPENDIX

THE FIG TREE [1]

I WANT shortly to answer the interesting question about the passage recording the cursing of the Fig Tree. I regard this as a tradition of secondary value. I cannot bring it into unity with the general picture of Jesus which tradition gives us. Jesus could not expect in spring to find ripe figs on a tree. Even if it had been the right time for ripe figs, and He had found the tree without fruit, His reported attitude towards this part of God's creation cannot be understood. To destroy a fruit tree without necessity appears to me to be actually sinful. I may perhaps here introduce a short story of an experience with a fig tree which I myself had. Years ago in the beautiful Rhine country, my mother had grown a fig tree from a cutting. When she had to leave the house on the death of my father, she gave me the fig tree. At that time I was professor in Heidelberg, and the tree often bore fruit. The tree was growing in a tub. I took it with me to Berlin, and could every year at the middle of February bring a twig of it to show to the students when I discussed the parable of the Fig Tree: " When her branch is yet tender, and putteth forth leaves, ye know that summer

---

[1] After the second lecture, in which Dr. Deissmann had incidentally referred to Matt. 21. 21, which occurs in the passage about Jesus cursing the fig tree, he was asked by a lady in the audience if he could explain the incident. This he did at the end of the third lecture. [Note by the translator.]

AND THE FAITH OF PAUL

is near."[1] At that time the twigs always bore their first green shoots. Then one hard winter, the tree was frozen. To me that was a very sad experience, because the tree was connected with some of the most beautiful years of my youth. Since that time it has become to me even more difficult to accept that Jesus could have destroyed a fig tree, simply because at a time when it could not have any fruit it did not have any.

The passage about the cursing of the Fig Tree seems therefore to me to be a secondary tradition, and stands at the end of a long development which I should like shortly to sketch to you.

First stage: Jesus wished to make clear to His disciples what faith is, and in doing so spoke the paradoxical word: "If ye had faith as a grain of mustard seed, ye might say unto this sycamine tree, Be thou plucked up by the roots, and be thou planted in the sea, and it should obey you." [2]

Second stage: On another occasion, He went beyond even this paradoxical word about the transplanting of a tree: "Verily I say unto you, if ye have faith and doubt not, ye shall not only do that about the fig tree, but also if ye shall say unto this mountain, be thou removed and be thou cast into the sea, it shall be done."[3] I have here in general followed the Authorised Version, with the one exception that in the middle of the sentence I have translated τὸ τῆς συκῆς word for word. I have translated it "that about the fig tree," which is the literal English translation.

Third stage: When later people quoted this saying, "Ye shall not only do this about the fig tree," they began to ask what Jesus had meant, and popular opinion

---

[1] Mark 13. 28.   [2] Luke 17. 6.   [3] Matt. 21. 21.

at once leapt to the conclusion that there had been a miracle. No doubt, also, the earlier parable of Jesus about the unfruitful fig tree,[1] which was planted in a vineyard, and about which there was a discussion between the master of the vineyard and the gardener, whether it should be cut down or not, had been applied popularly to the hardness of heart of Israel. And I think that from thinking over this, the idea had come about that Jesus had destroyed an unfruitful fig tree to symbolise the coming judgment on the unfruitful people of Israel.

---

[1] Luke 13. 6-9.

IV

THE WORKING OUT OF COMMUNION WITH GOD IN THE MESSAGE OF THE KINGDOM

As we spoke, in the last lecture, of the communion of Jesus with God the Father and God the Lord, we were looking at His general religious attitude, His personal religion in a state of rest. This normal, quiet piety of Jesus, is in all essentials similar to the best piety of His Jewish ancestors. It did not form any new theological terms, and itself had no consciousness of being anything new. But for all that, it is not simply identical with Jewish piety ; it is rather its vitalisation and intensification. One can understand this piety when one sees that Jesus spoke of God with the same words as thousands before Him, and thousands around Him. The difference consists in this, that He took quite seriously what to others had been simply words.

One has thus to picture the first three decades of His life as inwardly vitalised by this normal, quiet piety of communion with God the Father and God the Lord.

It is after these years that we see what was peculiar to Him. The normal, quiet piety develops into a historical activity, and this piety, becoming active and developing into action, is the starting-point of a spiritual movement that, from that time, has given its soul to nearly two thousand years of human culture. We shall see in the last lecture that we are here concerned with an action of Jesus that was, in fact, a reaction of His induced by the action of God.[1]

* * *

A significant word, a name of power has since the earliest tradition been attached to this prophetic activity of Jesus. It has been called εὐαγγέλιον (Evangelium), a word that is one of the greatest creations of mankind.

What is " Evangelium " ? Let me say here that the English language in the word

[1] *On Acting and Re-acting Mysticism*, see Part II, p. 195 ff., *infra*.

"Gospel" possesses a word that is the best and shortest equivalent for this word that I know. The possession of this word is one of the great spiritual values that have been committed to English-speaking Christianity. This word "Gospel" reflects a large part of the history of missions in Western countries. The word is found, as is known to you, first in the form "godspell"; Murray's Oxford Dictionary cites as the oldest reference, the Lindisfarne Gospels, about 950. It is practically certain that by "godspell" originally "good spell" was intended, that is, "good tidings," "gute Zeitung," as Luther occasionally translated. As a matter of fact in early times the first part of the word "godspell" was confused with "God," and the word was explained as meaning: "God tidings," possibly either "tidings about God" or "tidings from God." In this misunderstood form, the word was taken over by the missionaries from the Old English into other Germanic languages. In the Old Saxon in the form "godspell," in old High German in the form "gotspell," in the Old Norse (old

Icelandic) " godspiall." I wish, however, to repeat, so that there may not be any misunderstanding, that Gospel really means " good spell " : " good tidings." So your word " Gospel " has for us a homelike sound, though we unfortunately no more possess it ourselves, for both constituent parts of it, " god " and " spell," are Germanic words which continue to exist among us—the word " spell," for example, in the word " Beispiel."

The word " Evangelium " was not invented by primitive Christianity. It frequently occurred in the ancient world, and had, as the inscriptions and papyri show, already received a religious note in relation to the Emperor-worship.

What does the New Testament understand by " Evangelium " ? I cannot ask this question without thinking of the great controversy which we have had in Germany in the last few decades on this word, both in our synods, as we deliberated about our new church constitution in recent years, and also in scientific theology. I would remind you of the dispute over Harnack's formula of the "double

Evangelium." In all these conflicts, a broader and a narrower meaning of the word " Evangelium " stood in the background. Many understood by " Gospel " the whole content of the New Testament, or the whole primitive Christology, or the message of the free grace of God in Christ Jesus. In all these cases, we can observe an extension of the primitive idea of " Evangelium." All these definitions are not, so to say, false ; but they reflect later stages of the development of the idea. The word " Evangelium " is such a living word, that even up to the present day it has not come to be a stereotyped expression. Even in our own time, it has acquired new shades of meaning.

The question about the earliest meaning of the word " Evangelium " within the New Testament, is not difficult to answer. " Evangelium " is " the glad tidings (of the Kingdom of God) announced by Jesus Christ." This definition, given by the Oxford English Dictionary, is perfectly correct. The word " Gospel " has, in the original use, this quite restricted meaning : the message of good tidings of the Kingdom of God. From this all the other meanings have since developed, even the one that is so common with us, according to which " Gospel " is equivalent to " book of the Gospel."

" Glad " tidings of the Kingdom of God—this sense of the word is particularly understandable if one recollects the historical situation. " The people that sat in darkness " could not have understood the message of the Kingdom of God otherwise than as a good message, and so in the word " Gospel " there still remains something of the passionate excitement and joy of an oppressed people who first heard the message of the coming Kingdom.

In this message of the Kingdom we see the historical working out of the communion of Jesus with God, and this message of His we have now to endeavour to understand. But first, we must look for a moment at the development of the idea in later times.

* * *

The idea of the Kingdom of God has passed through a varied development in the history of Christianity. This history of the development of the idea of the Kingdom of God from Jesus down to the present day is a subject which ought to be investigated on the grand scale, for it would reflect a considerable portion of the inner history of Christianity. In particular it would be seen how Christian thinkers have fitted the idea of the Kingdom of God to current systems of philosophy. So in each age the idea of the Kingdom of God has been modernised, and not infrequently it has been violently altered, especially when the attempt has been made to compress it into certain theological systems.

If we wish to understand the real hope of the Kingdom which Jesus held, we must not adopt *a priori* any of these varied developments in history of the idea of the Kingdom as set forth by Jesus, although they still have a great influence in preaching and in explanation in commentaries. If we want to discover the working out of communion with God in Christ's message of the Kingdom we must view it in its essential relation to its historical pre-conditions.

* * *

The historical presupposition of the preaching of the Kingdom both of the Baptist and of Jesus is the Old Testament and Jewish idea of a kingly rule of God. This kingly rule of God is indeed always at hand in the present, but in the future it will come to its own in a particularly concentrated and effective manner. People hoped in the future for a coming state of things in which the people of Israel would become a theocracy under a God-anointed king, a theocracy which would only be possible through a divine miracle. This hope is closely related to the late Jewish expectation of the coming æon.[1] Sometimes the hope had materialistic and sometimes spiritual features. It became especially passionate during the time of oppression under Roman rule.

The message of the Kingdom in the teaching of Jesus has come to us only in Greek translation. There are two questions which must be answered before we can go further. First, is there a real distinction between " Kingdom of Heaven " in Matthew, and " Kingdom of

[1] αἰὼν ἐρχόμενος.

God " in the other evangelists ? This question is to be answered in the negative. " Heaven " is metonymy for God.[1] It is not improbable that Jesus used the two expressions promiscuously. The expression " Kingdom of Heaven " is more intimate and more homelike in Palestine. In the world without it might not have been so easily understood, and for that reason the expression " Kingdom of God " has later become customary. The expression " Kingdom of Heaven " afterwards and up to the present day has been in innumerable cases referred to the other world in eternity. It is from this that one of the most important changes of meaning in the idea of the Kingdom is to be understood, the transferring of the Kingdom from this world into the other world. But if one is to understand Jesus, one must not start from that point of view. " Kingdom of Heaven " is for Him the same as " Kingdom of God."

[1] Cf. the parable of the Prodigal Son, Luke 15. 18 and 21 ; and the Jewish expression *malkuth shamajim*, which seems to be entirely parallel in meaning to *malkuth Jahweh*.

Secondly, is the Greek word which is translated in the English Bible " Kingdom " really to be translated best " Kingdom " or " Sovereignty " ? The second, the dynamic, understanding of the word is to be preferred, in most cases, to the local idea conveyed by the first, which in Greek is in general the more unusual.

The answering of the question of how Jesus used the word " Kingdom " is often made difficult by dogmatic attitudes towards the history. As already indicated, modernisation of the idea has considerably influenced the interpretation, but the whole method of putting the question has frequently hindered the gaining of a true answer. The thought of the Kingdom has been handled as if it were a technical idea out of a philosophic system. People have questioned about the conception of the Kingdom as Jesus used it in the same way that they have questioned about the conception of the Platonic idea, or the concept of satisfaction according to Anselm, or the conception of the categorical imperative in Kant. They have sought an idea that has always exactly the same meaning, which could be fitted into a dogmatic or ethical system. In the formulation of the theme, the working out of communion with God in the message of the Kingdom, there lies a protest against this method. We must try to understand the hope of the Kingdom as a living part of the inner experience of Jesus, as varying reflections of His communion with God, and therefore I venture to state that we cannot really define the consciousness of the Kingdom of God in the sayings of Jesus. As soon as one reaches a " definition " with regard to these ultimate and most delicate things in the spiritual world, one has ruined them. The " definition " of the idea of the Kingdom can only be performed on an anatomical method. We have rather to work biologically. The hope of the Kingdom which Jesus held was something living, which was capable of widely differing contents and moods.

What are these different moods of the hope of the Kingdom according to Jesus ? We can almost everywhere observe, on the one hand, a mood that is related to the Jewish understanding of the Kingdom, and, on the other hand, a mood which goes far beyond anything that the Jews thought of. The thought of the Kingdom according to Jesus floats between these two poles, and we have probably found a good methodological thought, if we speak of the polarity in His idea of the Kingdom.

Entirely in harmony with the ancestral hope, He views the Kingdom as a new order of things upon earth, which after the expiration of the present period of the world, already on the way to its speedy downfall, will be brought in by God. The Kingdom is not " of " this world, *i.e.* it does not come from the present sinful, evil age of the world, but from God. Yet it comes upon this earth. Jesus in bold, virile trust on His God did not abandon the earth to eternal misery, but saw a renewed earth upon which God reigned over redeemed, sanctified, good men. That is the ground why the indispensable pre-condition for participation in this Kingdom is change of mind, repentance.[1] With this ethical strengthening of the idea of the Kingdom, Jesus is raised high above the popular expectation.

[1] μετάνοια.

AND THE FAITH OF PAUL

On this point, we have to note a passage in the Bible that has been the cause of serious misunderstanding. I refer to John 18. 26: " My kingdom is not of this world." Many people on the Continent, and I should gather also in England, understand this saying as follows : " The Kingdom of God is a purely other-worldly matter, and has nothing to do with the things of this world." And so this saying has become a cudgel, with which the social reformer and politician, who regards himself as standing on the ground of the Gospel, may be struck down. But the meaning of the expression here is quite different. The Greek text [1] means that the origin of the Kingdom of God is not from this world— that is, not from the world which is under the rule of Satan—but from the other world, God's world, and this implies that the Kingdom of God is to come *from* the world of God, *into* the world of Satan.

Here again it may be pointed out that the misunderstood phrase " Kingdom of Heaven " has greatly contributed to make the applica-

[1] ἡ βασιλεία ἡ ἐμὴ οὐκ ἔστιν ἐκ τοῦ κόσμου τούτου.

tion of the Kingdom of God to this world unrecognised. Many a Christian, to whom Christianity is entirely a delicate inner attitude of the soul, is shocked when he hears that the Kingdom of God means an immense revolution in this world. But we must recognise the tremendous fact that Christianity is both an inner attitude of the individual soul and a programme of revolution for the world. It appears to me historically to be quite certain that Jesus shared in the powerful, popular expectation of the Kingdom. But certainly He ennobled all that was sensually common in this expectation. His " Kingdom of God is not meat and drink." This Pauline saying [1] might easily be a quotation from a word of Jesus Himself. We can make His position, and His relation to the popular idea of the Kingdom clear to ourselves through a simile. He grafted ethical demands into the wild stock of the popular hope of the Kingdom. So His Kingdom of God does not mean a fantastic, sensual Mohammedan heaven on earth, but a humanity led by God Himself,

[1] Rom. 14. 17.

AND THE FAITH OF PAUL 115

because it has been transformed by God Himself.

As for the religion of His ancestors, so for Jesus, the Kingdom is the object of His hope. The Kingdom comes, the Kingdom is near. But it is not merely future. Jesus had moments in which, standing before the cornfield growing green, He already saw the day of the harvest dawning. From this it comes to pass, that His hope of the Kingdom, though it is in no sense the programme of a cleverly calculating party leader, but a prophetic certainty, still has nothing about it fantastically exciting. Clumsy tokens for the beginning of the Kingdom, there are none. As the seed grows, unnoticed, gradually, from small beginnings, so comes the Kingdom, like a grain of mustard seed, like leaven.

With these suggestions, I have touched upon a problem which used to be passionately discussed in the last generation. Some amongst us will remember the impressive experience they had, when first they realised that the Kingdom, according to Jesus, was something that was coming. We had long become accustomed to the comfortable idea that the Kingdom of God had for a long time been present, that it was established by Jesus Himself, and that we had simply to join ourselves to it by faith. I regard it as a great service rendered by the newer study of the Bible, that it strongly emphasised the coming character of the Kingdom according to Jesus. The great majority of the sayings about the Kingdom refer to its coming. Jesus certainly believed that God already ruled the world as King, but He expected a quite special act of God, by which the definite Kingdom of God would be set up in the world. In moments of special prophetic insight He occasionally saw this coming Kingdom as if it were already present. I give one instance : " The Kingdom of God is within you." [1] These words were said to the Pharisees. They do not mean, therefore, " You have already in your heart the Kingdom of God," as though the Kingdom of God was a hidden, inward affair; the expression " within you " rather means, as the Revised Version translates it in the margin, " in the

[1] Luke 17. 21 : ἡ βασιλεία τοῦ θεοῦ ἐντὸς ὑμῶν ἐστιν.

midst of you," and Jesus here thinks, in that moment of highest prophetic insight, of Himself as the already present, visible, representative of the Kingdom of God. We have here then a case of prophetic anticipation.

Like His own people, Jesus expected the Kingdom as a reward for the righteous. In particular, He expected with the coming of the Kingdom the great compensation, which brings to the poor, the oppressed, the persecuted and the humble, all which till that time had been withheld from them ; but the popular, legal idea of reward is in His mind deepened into the glorious conception of a gift of grace. The Kingdom is reward, but it is not to be gained by merit. The message of the Kingdom is comfort, but it is also earnest warning. He who listens only for the harps of peace from it, will be shaken to the very marrow by the trumpet tones of the day of wrath, with its terrible separation of the evil from the good.

The whole earnestness of His expectation of the Kingdom is indicated by this fact, that He set the old Jewish idea of judgment in the centre of His picture of the Kingdom. For

Him also, then, the Kingdom of God is equally gift and task, comfort and warning at the same time. It seems to me that in this union of religious warmth and ethical seriousness, we can see particularly clearly the working out of the communion with God the Father and God the Lord.

The Kingdom is the inheritance of Israel. This popular hope is the starting point for Jesus also. But the national barrier was broken through for Him by the unexpectedly magnificent experience of the confident faith of a Gentile.[1] He saw the Kingdom as something for all mankind. So the message of the Kingdom, according to Jesus, contained a great programme of home mission and foreign mission.

This last case may perhaps enable us psychologically to understand the peculiar oscillation in the hope of the Kingdom as the result of outer and inner experiences. I do not regard it as wise to speak of a development of the idea of the Kingdom in the thoughts of Jesus, as though He had had at the first a

[1] Matt. 8. 10.

home mission programme, and it then "developed" into a foreign mission programme. I do not think, either, that the expressions "dualism" or "antinomy" properly apply to the position of Jesus. These two words do not solve the problem—they merely state it, or conceal it. One would rather adopt the simile, which Holtzmann used, of an ellipse with two foci; or we might, as before, speak of a polarity of the thought of the Kingdom according to Jesus.

* * *

The importance for the history of religion of the prophecy of the Kingdom according to Jesus consists in this: that in it the quiet, normal piety of Jesus blazes up into a great flame. At this point, we at once see that the last problem, the problem of His Messiahship comes to the front. This we have to discuss in the next lecture.

The prophecy of the Kingdom by Jesus had one peculiar historical effect, that it originated the movement out of which all that we call "primitive Christianity" and Christianity all together, came. It first powerfully shook the masses, and filled them with Messianic fervour. It separated from this multitude a little body of followers of Jesus, who formed the nucleus of the future Christian community. It carried the conflict of Jesus with the rulers to His martyrdom and His cross, and it then became one of the driving forces of the Christ cult. In the single prayer that has come to us from the primitive community, in its Aramaic mother language, Marana tha (" Come, our Lord "), quivers the old expectation of the coming of the Kingdom, now concentrated upon the coming of the Lord Himself.

In the dogmatic and ethical thought of later Christianity, the thought of the Kingdom has exhibited a great elasticity and power of adaptation. I have already indicated something of this development of the idea within the Christian Church, and will therefore say nothing further about it here.

But one word must still be said about the value for us of the message of the Kingdom according to Jesus. It is extraordinarily

AND THE FAITH OF PAUL 121

great. In the first place, it vitalises for us, in the strongest form, the consciousness which Jesus Himself had of God, and reveals to us what God really is, combining kindness and holiness. Of as great importance is the prophecy of the Kingdom according to Jesus, as a mirror of Jesus Himself. And lastly, it seems to me that two pieces of knowledge, for which we have to thank the newer scholarship, are of the greatest importance for the present day.

The two pieces of knowledge are these: First, that the Kingdom of God is not something finished and ready for us, but an immense task for the present and future. The Kingdom is still to come. The second is this: the Kingdom of God is not simply a matter of the other world, but is a new condition of affairs in this world, produced by power from the other world.

In both there lies a great programme, of home and foreign mission, and of international work, both political and social. If Christianity of to-day adopted the expectation of the Kingdom which Jesus had, then it would be, not only a venerable phenomenon out of the past, and its spiritual power would not need to be exhausted in retrospective, dogmatical work, but it would be the voice of one crying in the wilderness of this our time, pointing forward to the great goal of God for humanity.

Those among the younger of my hearers who have the purpose of co-operating towards this goal, in teaching, social, missionary and international work, can quite simply make clear to themselves the meaning of the Kingdom of God according to Jesus, if they, as they enter upon their field of work, say: " Here, where I am going to work, the Kingdom of God is not yet present ; it is to come, and it ought to come here in this place." It is in this attitude of mind that every one of us should pray the second petition of the Lord's Prayer : " Thy Kingdom come ! "

V

THE DYNAMIC CULMINATION OF COMMUNION WITH GOD IN JESUS' CONSCIOUSNESS OF MISSION AND MESSIAHSHIP. WHAT NEW THING DID JESUS BRING?

WE have sought to grasp the message of Jesus about the Kingdom of God, as the working out of His communion with God. The normal, quiet piety of Jesus develops into an historical activity; and we have already suggested that we are here concerned with an action of Jesus that was, in fact, a reaction of His, induced by the action of God. Seen by the eyes of Jesus Himself, what we call the consciousness of Mission and Messiahship is an action of God Himself.

The great message of the Kingdom of God stands in the closest connection with this secret of His inner life. If we dare to speak of this to-day, we must from the very first admit that it is finally a secret, and that our historical instruments do not avail to solve it. Yet it has often been regarded as if it were a comparatively easy problem, and the great difficulties with which one is faced perhaps arise from the fact that the matter has been considered too easy, that an immediate and simple answer has been sought, when the narrow limitations of our knowledge ought to have been recognised.

I would draw attention in particular to one point. The great difficulties that the Messianic consciousness of Jesus holds for the newer investigation have to a considerable extent arisen thus ; the attempt has been made by means of doctrinaire methods of questioning to grasp the secret of His inner life. Now, it appears to me to be entirely impossible to consider the Messianic consciousness of Jesus within a system of the " teaching "of Jesus, in at all the way in which, for instance, one might discuss : What did Jesus teach about God ? What did He teach about sin ? and so on, down to the last question : What did He teach about Himself ? I remember a highly gifted friend and colleague, who said to me once in conversation on this question : If Jesus really did teach these things, then He must have been a visionary. His view was that the expressions of Messianic consciousness had been attributed to Him later by the Church. To his careful and systematic mind, they appeared like something foreign to the system.

If one wishes to understand the Messianic consciousness of Jesus (I mean in so far as anyone can understand such a thing) one must in some way or other see it from the point of view of His communion with God, and further one must not historically isolate the Messianic consciousness of Jesus, but look at it in connection with His consciousness of His Mission as the oldest tradition indicates.[1] The two, the consciousness of Mission and the consciousness of His Messiahship, must be grasped together as the culmination of His communion with God.

The inner life of Jesus, in His communion with God, appears to me to have three stages. The basal groundwork is the quiet piety of His communion with God the Father and

[1] Luke 4. 18.

God the Lord; to this there comes, as a specific consciousness, a consciousness of prophetic endowment for His Mission; and, finally, the prophetic consciousness culminates in the Messianic consciousness.

The peculiarity of the prophetic consciousness is this, that the consciousness of communion with God is concentrated in the consciousness of a specific divine act. Jesus is conscious of being sent. He Himself speaks of it thus: " I must preach the good tidings of the Kingdom of God to the other cities also, for therefore I was sent." [1] In this passage, the " I must " is just as important to the understanding of His prophetic consciousness as the " I am sent." In the same way, " I was not sent but unto the lost sheep of the house of Israel," [2] and : " And he that receiveth me, receiveth Him that sent me." [3] In the Gospel of John we have the strong echo of this " I am sent."

A complementary idea is expressed in the words " I am come," about which I would refer you to the fine study of Harnack, *Ich*

[1] Luke 4. 43.   [2] Matt. 15. 24.   [3] Matt. 10. 40.

AND THE FAITH OF PAUL

bin gekommen. The most important passages for this are Matt. 10. 34 ff., Mark 2. 17, Mark 10. 45, Luke 12. 49, 50, Luke 19. 10, Luke 9. 56,[1] and Matthew 5. 17. The word "I," so strongly emphasised in some sayings, also points back to this prophetic consciousness; for example, the mighty words of the Sermon on the Mount: "But I say unto you,"[2] and "Behold I send you forth as sheep in the midst of wolves."[3] In the Gospel of John we have a further development of this, in the use of the phrase "I am," which has undoubtedly been influenced by sacred usage.

Also the turn of phrase, "Here is a greater than . . ." points to the same consciousness. "A greater than Jonah is here," and "A greater than Solomon is here,"[4] and "One greater than the Temple is here."[5] I may here perhaps add that the Johannine "Before Abraham was, I am" is to be understood, not

---

[1] As it stands in the Authorised English Version and in many ancient MSS. and versions.
[2] Matt. 5. 22, 28, 34, 39, 44.   [3] Matt. 10. 16.
[4] Matt. 12. 41, 42.   [5] Matt. 12. 6.

in the ordinary chronological sense, but in sense of value.[1] Because Jesus had this consciousness of a special mission, He demanded unheard-of sacrifices from His followers. The short stories, Luke 9. 57 to 62, are of special importance on this point. They belong to the most valuable indirect testimonies to His consciousness of mission, and are throughout upon the level expressed in the saying: " He that loveth father or mother more than me, is not worthy of me ; and he that loveth son or daughter more than me is not worthy of me." [2]

The impression that Jesus made on those about Him also throws a light on His prophetic consciousness. His opponents expressed it thus: " He blasphemeth " ; His followers said : " He taught as one having authority, and not as the scribes." [3] In this passage popular feeling had a true insight. It sees the great distance between the Scribes, the professionally religious, and the prophetic genius of Jesus, and the feeling is deeply

---

[1] John 8. 58.   [2] Matt. 10. 37.
[3] Matt. 7. 29, ὡς ἐξουσίαν ἔχων.

influenced by the divine authority of His Mission.

The question how this consciousness of His Mission arose in Jesus cannot be answered. In our sources it is something given. One can only suggest, as I said in an earlier lecture, that the appearance of John the Baptist, with his powerful prophecy, brought into the forefront of the consciousness of Jesus the sense of His own Mission ; that, in fact, the holy spark had leapt from the Baptist to Him.

The question also how the Messianic consciousness arose in the soul of Jesus cannot be answered. History has drawn a veil over the birth-hour of that momentous conviction. We have probably but one remaining reminiscence in the story of the Baptism. According to my view, the Gospel narratives of baptism go back to accounts that came from the lips of Jesus Himself. We have testimony that He gave to His disciples suggestions of such extraordinary experiences. A saying recorded by Luke only is here of special importance : " I beheld Satan fall as lightning from heaven."[1] In the same way, I think, He must have related to His disciples, that He, at the time of His baptism by John, saw the heavens opened and the Holy Spirit descending like a dove upon Him, and heard the voice of God: " Thou art my beloved Son. To-day I have begotten thee."[2] In my opinion, Mark has preserved the best tradition of the whole scene, and the heavenly voice was identical with the words of Psalm 2. 7. In the development of this story, we can trace the stages to the complete objectification of this experience of Jesus. In our scientific language we should call these experiences " visions " and " auditions." But in any case, however we may call them, they appear to be quite typical of what we have called in the title of this lecture " the dynamic culmination of communion with God." The consciousness long present that God was His Father, and He was God's child, increases in this moment to the certainty that He is *the* Son of God.

[1] Luke 10. 18.
[2] So the Western text of Luke's Gospel records the incident. Luke 3. 22.

This experience of the baptism, I regard as the first dawning of the Messianic consciousness of Jesus, and it is here most important that we should understand of what kind this Messianic consciousness is. I cannot believe that the Messianic consciousness of Jesus was the result of reflection or of a process of exegetical study, which then from the first beginnings of its appearance was His fixed and quiet possession. I picture to myself this consciousness of Jesus rather thus: that, as a consciousness given by God, it had its flow and ebb. It was not present with Him always with the same intensity. It is sometimes replaced by the merely prophetic consciousness. It is a consciousness that dawns, and then disappears, that blazes in heavenly clearness in great hours of revelation before which He then, however, draws back in humility and simplicity. He does not refuse to speak about such experiences to those He trusts, but almost as soon as He has spoken of them, He desires to hide them again. I regard the words to the disciples, that they must not speak about His Messiahship, in general as genuine.

The investigators, who had doubted the genuineness of these commands not to speak of the Messiahship, have not set the whole problem sufficiently clearly in its place in the religious history of the ancient world. The question " Am I the Messiah ? " was not a personal, perhaps quite interesting, question, about His future calling. It was not akin, for example, to the question whether He should in the near future, accept a famous professorship in a Jewish school. It was a life-and-death question. The religious history of the ancient world is not written with ink, but with blood, and it is to me very probable that for Jesus the question of Messiahship, and the question of suffering and death came up together ; and so I understand it, when He forbids the disciples to speak about it, that this prohibition is just as much a testimony to His own humility, as a proof that He did not wish to provoke His own martyrdom.

Tradition has preserved for us certain of those hours of revelation. Apart from the already mentioned accounts of the Baptism, I regard as the most important the scene in the Synagogue of His home city, Nazareth.[1] Jesus goes on the Sabbath to the Synagogue, and stands up to read. He unrolls the roll of the prophet given to Him, and, as if by accident, His eye falls on the words in Isaiah : " The Spirit of the Lord is upon me, because he anointed me to preach good tidings to the poor, He hath sent me to proclaim release to the captives, and recovering of sight to the blind, to set at liberty them that are bruised, to proclaim the acceptable year of the Lord." In the conviction that here His own anointing and sending is spoken of, He cries to the congregation : " To-day hath this Scripture been fulfilled in your ears." This, to my mind, exceptionally important passage can easily be misunderstood, by supposing that Jesus had come into the Synagogue with the purpose of reading the prophetic words, and announcing in connection with them that He was the Messiah. Rather, as His eye falls upon these words, " He anointed me, He hath sent me," the illumination comes to Him that He *is* the Anointed One.

[1] Luke 4. 16 ff.

For another reason also this passage is peculiarly important. It answers the question, How did Jesus regard His own Mission and Messiahship, how did He regard His anointing and sending? For Him, the Anointed of the Lord is not the militant, deliverer-king of popular expectation. When the picture of a Kingdom over the earth is presented to Him it is recognised as Satanic temptation.[1] His Messiah bears the features of the great merciful Saviour of the poor, the sick, the rejected and the prisoners, the lost, and in other testimonies the features of the Redeemer of sinners. Even in the awful pictures of the Day of Judgment [2] His Messiah seeks among the people, not bodyguards, secretaries of state, generals, but He asks for those who have fed the hungry, given drink to the thirsty, shelter to the strangers, clothed the naked, and have cared for the sick and prisoners. Thus His picture of the Messiah had less a national political, than a humane social, aspect.

* * *

[1] Matt. 4. 8 ff.   [2] Matt. 25. 31 ff.

The fact of Jesus' Messianic consciousness has been denied. These denials have been overvalued as regards their bearing upon Christian piety. There is among us an anxious apprehension, which thinks that present-day Christianity stands or falls according to the results of the investigation in theological faculties. But, surely, Christianity is carried along by a divine energy that works within it, not by the results of scientific investigation. The peculiar power of the personality of Jesus is not dependent on whether He did as a matter of fact claim to be Messiah or not. The idea of Messiahship is, indeed, from the very beginning a specifically Jewish idea, and as a matter of fact at once fell decidedly into the background when Christianity left its first home and passed over into the sphere of a world religion. The history of the word " Christos " shews this particularly clearly. " Christos," in the beginning the translation of the Semitic word " Messiah," gradually became a proper name, precisely as the name " The Buddha," away from its original home, almost always is understood as a proper name. In world-wide Christianity, outside Judæa, the conception of " Messiah " very soon gave way to the conception of " Lord."

For that reason I do not believe that the solution of this question has a decisive value for present-day Christian piety. The Christian Church would still throng round Jesus as Lord, even if there were adequate grounds for denying that He possessed the Messianic consciousness. But within the sphere of theological discussion, the question is of course of the very greatest moment; and here I think that the denial of the Messianic consciousness of Jesus has not been, in any sense, a step forward in theological science.

To doubt that He possessed it is only possible when one treats the sources with violence. I would like, here again, to draw attention to the importance of the account of the preaching in the Synagogue at Nazareth.[1] This passage is one of the strongest witnesses for the consciousness of Messiahship in Jesus.

[1] Luke 4. 16 ff.

That is, of course, if it is taken in the sense in which I have dealt with it.

That many sayings of Jesus are simply generally prophetic, rather than specifically Messianic, is quite certain; and we might understand His message of the Kingdom of God, which was taken over from the message of John, simply as prophetic. It is also fully to be admitted that Jesus can be understood in the religious-historical sense only as He is brought into close contact with the prophets. But for all that, the prophet Jesus did not feel Himself to be simply a prophet following the prophets. To His " greater than Jonah "[1] is also to be added the fact that from John himself He is separated by something new.[2] With John, Jesus finally closes the old, the epoch of the Law and the Prophets; with His own Mission begins the new, the acceptable year of the Lord, the harvest of God, the Messianic time. This dividing off from John and the old epoch, is by so much more remarkable, as Jesus, apart from that, gave an extraordinarily high place to the Baptist.

[1] Matt. 12. 41.   [2] Matt. 11. 11-13.

Along with this dividing off of the epochs, we reckon the already mentioned testimonies to an " I "-consciousness, that goes far beyond anything merely prophetic.

Of great importance, too, is the confirmation which Jesus gave to Peter's confession.[1] To the testimony, " Thou art the Christ, the son of the living God," Jesus replied, " Blessed art thou, Simon Barjona, for flesh and blood hath not revealed it unto thee, but my Father which is in Heaven." I have strong doubts about the genuineness of the following verse : " Thou art Peter, and upon this rock I will build my church." But the word addressed to Peter, which I have just quoted, appears to me to be genuine. From these words by the method of indirect observation, one can deduce how Jesus may have come to His consciousness of Messiahship ; it too was by revelation from God.

The question what Jesus answered to the High Priest at His trial, is extraordinarily difficult, for the tradition is not unanimous. According to Matthew, Jesus answered to

[1] Matt. 16. 16 ff.

AND THE FAITH OF PAUL

the question of the High Priest if He were the Messiah: "Thou hast said."[1] We have been accustomed to understand this "Thou hast said" as an affirmative, but according to the Greek text one must emphasise, not the word "said," but the word "thou," for it is the pronoun which is emphatic. So also in the parallel report by Luke: "*Ye* say that I am."[2] In the same way, before Pilate, "*Thou* sayest,"[3] and similarly in the parallels of Mark and Luke.[4] If one had only these traditions, one would have to say that Jesus neither affirmed nor denied His Messiahship, when asked about it by the High Priest. He rather refused to answer. He, at the most, gave an indirect answer with the words: "Nevertheless I say unto you, hereafter shall ye see the Son of Man, sitting on the right hand of power, and coming in the clouds of Heaven." That even in very early times the answer He gave was understood as an affirmative is shown by Mark's report of

---

[1] Matt. 26. 64, σὺ εἶπας.
[2] Luke 22. 70, ὑμεῖς λέγετε, ὅτι ἐγώ εἰμι.
[3] Matt. 27. 11, σύ λέγεις.   [4] Mark 15. 2; Luke 23. 3.

His answer: "And Jesus said, I am, and ye shall see the Son of Man sitting on the right hand of power, and coming in the clouds of heaven."[1] I would therefore lay no decisive weight on these passages, but the other passages in my opinion are sufficient.

The question whether in the consciousness of Jesus the Messiahship was regarded as something present or as something still future is dependent upon the answering of the question whether the Kingdom of God is present or future. In general, the Messianic consciousness, like the message of the Kingdom of God, referred to the future. But in moments of especial inspiration He experienced this future Messiahship as already present.

Certain special names for the Messiah which Jesus used require to be mentioned: the expressions "Son of David," "Son of God," and "Son of Man." Jesus was, according to good traditions,[2] the son of a family descended from David. He seems Himself, however, to have laid little weight

[1] Mark 14. 62.   [2] Cf. Rom. 1. 3.

on the fact of His Davidic descent, and on the name " David's son." When one looks at the famous passage, " How say the scribes that the Christ is the Son of David ? "[1] and rightly understands it, one may deduce from it that Jesus held the Messianic title " Son of David " as one of small value. According to Semitic and general human understanding, a son is regarded as subordinate to his father, and so in the title " Son of David " the thought must lie that the Messiah is something less than David. Against this, the conviction of Jesus protests. Jesus recognises in Psalm 110 that the Messiah is the Lord of David, and so one might write under this famous Son-of-David passage, " Here is one greater than David."

The Messianic title " Son of God," which was probably derived from Psalm 2, was in the Gospel tradition frequently used in the mouth of the people, and it was no doubt understood as Messianic by Jesus when He heard the heavenly voice at His Baptism.

The title " Son of Man " finally seems to

[1] Mark 12. 35.

have been a favourite one in the use of Jesus. I cannot agree with the hypothesis that it was put into His mouth by a later generation, for we find it is exactly in the later generations that this title of the Messiah has gone entirely out of use. The title was quite specially Jewish, and could not have been understood by Gentile Christians outside Palestine. So much so was this the case, that the Epistle of Barnabas protests against the use of Son of Man as a title of Jesus.[1] Only in the Gospel of John, where there is a great conflict with the Jews, does the title retain great importance in later days. I regard it as quite unlikely that a title which was so little used in later times could have been in those later times first attributed to Jesus.

The matter seems to me rather to be thus: that Jesus had taken over a Jewish title, already coined. It appears that even before Jesus, the passage Daniel 7. 13, which from the first was not intended Messianically, had been understood Messianically. Jesus Him-

[1] Barnabas 12. 10.

self quoted the passage, and understood it Messianically.[1] In several places in the Greek tradition of the sayings of Jesus, where Jesus speaks of "man" in the Aramaic Bar-nasha, the Greek translators have understood it Messianically, and rendered it "the Son of Man."[2] I believe this is the case in the passage, "The Sabbath was made for man, and not man for the Sabbath: therefore the Son of man is Lord also of the Sabbath."[3] I think the better translation of the original Aramaic saying would be: "The Sabbath was made for man, and not man for Sabbath; therefore man is lord also of the Sabbath," and so this saying would not belong to the Messianic testimonies of Jesus.

* * *

Wherein lies the historical importance of the Messianic consciousness of Jesus? One might, after what has been said, possibly assume that the whole Messianic idea was only a small matter that had no importance, except for Jewish Christians. But to pass

[1] Matt. 24. 30, and 26. 64. [2] ὁ υἱὸς τοῦ ἀνθρώπου.
[3] Mark 2. 27, 28.

such a verdict would be a great mistake. The Messianic consciousness of Jesus has results of the greatest importance for the general development of Christianity.

In the first place, the Messianic consciousness of Jesus was the cause of His conflict with the ruling powers, and therefore of His passion and Cross. So the Messianic consciousness of Jesus is one of the pre-conditions of the enormous thought-development, which has been linked on to His passion and death.

Secondly, the Messianic consciousness of Jesus was ultimately the cause of the formation of a new religious community. Jesus did not Himself come forward with the intention of forming a new community. He lived Himself within the organisation of the Synagogue, and, when He prophesied to the disciples that they would be driven out of the Synagogue, He accepted, as the natural condition of things, that their home was in the Synagogue.[1]

[1] It is of the Synagogue congregation that the saying Matt. 18. 17 is to be understood. The passage Matt. 16. 16, on the other hand, I regard on several grounds as secondary.

At first, only a sort of community of personal followers, without organisation, had gathered itself round Him, and the first beginning of any special marking out of this circle is the Lord's Prayer. But the possession of this prayer did not imply that the disciples of Jesus were separated from the Jewish community. The stronger, however, the Messianic consciousness of Jesus became, and the more the disciples held Him Himself to be the Messiah, so much the more was there a growth of opposition against those who denied His Messiahship. So far the Messianic consciousness of Jesus had a great importance in preparing for the coming Christian Church. The Messianic claim of Jesus, in its origin entirely Jewish, became the cause of a universal new religious formation. Jesus, probably, if it had not been for His Messianic claim, would have stood in the Talmud along with the other great Rabbis, Hillel and Gamaliel. Jesus the Messiah is the sign which is spoken against,[1] and it was through this contradiction that Christianity

[1] Luke 2. 34.

as a new religious formation came into being.

Thirdly, the consciousness of Messiahship in Jesus, and the belief of His disciples in His Messiahship, directed attention to His Person, and although Jesus the Messiah became more and more Jesus Christ, even so it was the Messiah idea that gave the force which carried the Person of Christ into the centre of Christianity. The Messiah idea is the pre-condition required to produce from the so-called " Christianity of Christ," Christ-Christianity, or the Christ-cult. No doubt, this centralising upon the Person of Jesus had some unhealthy effects in the times that followed. A soul-less speculation made itself master of the Person of Christ, and revelled in the problems of a Christology, inwardly foreign to the Gospel. It divided the children of God, and the fellow-heirs with Christ, in bloody battles over the inheritance. But by such evil results, the centralisation of the Person of Christ must not be judged.

These evil effects were richly compensated for by a fourth result. The centralisation of

Christianity on the Person of Jesus is of the greatest importance in the development of Christianity as a religion of the people. Christianity does not gather mankind together round a system of religious theories, but round a divine personality. If Christianity were the content of a theoretic system, then it would have to be judged as the Welt-Anschauung of a small intellectual circle. But the concentration of religious feeling on a personality makes possible the evangelisation of the world, of mankind in all its varying strata and stages of culture.

What is characteristic to-day in the great complexity of Christian mankind is not doctrine, which rather emphasises differences, but the power in extensive and intensive working that the communion of Jesus with God has from generation to generation.

From this point, then, we reach the last standpoint for the answering of the question : What new thing did Jesus bring ? This setting of the question is a favourite one, and a great mass of intellectual power maintains that it is His " teaching " which was the new thing He brought. Especially in discussions with Jewish theology, it has been sought to prove that Christ brought a new idea of God, or a new teaching of the Kingdom of God, or that the new was His command of love to the neighbour. If He Himself could be asked about these suggested points, He would very possibly answer that He made no claim to teach anything new. He would perhaps say that He came to bring the old to its own, just as, as a matter of fact, He did say that He came to " fulfil the law and the prophets."[1] There are, indeed, new doctrines in His sayings, and that not in small number. But on the whole, His connection with the religion of His fathers is very intimate. And so I think we must transfer the question, what new thing Jesus brought, from the doctrinaire ground to another. We must look at the question entirely as a dynamic matter, and I believe in this way we shall stand on the same ground as the oldest

[1] Matt. 5. 17.

Christian verdict in the matter. His earliest disciples had the impression of a new teaching, but a new teaching with authority.[1] "For He taught them as one having authority, and not as the scribes."[2]

Had Jesus been a Scribe, then it would be the right thing to ask about His teaching; but because Jesus is Jesus, one should ask rather about authority. And so I would say that the originality of Jesus lies in His whole personality, in the peculiar energy of His experience of the living God. It is not His concepts that are original, but His power; not His formulæ, but His confessions; not His dogmas, but His faith; not His system, but His personality. The originality of Jesus lies in the comprehensive uniqueness of His inner life; the new, the epoch-making thing, is Himself.

The peculiar thing is not, that there were to be found, on His string of pearls, twelve or twenty of such size as had never before been seen, but that in the treasure-chamber of the religions of mankind there is this one

---

[1] Mark 1. 27. [2] Matt. 7. 29.

diamond, which sheds forth rays of such unexampled fire and purity.

With this statement, I come upon the same ground as many others, of whom I will only mention two: Adolf von Harnack and Julius Wellhausen. But already in the earliest times of Christian theology, this same statement is presented to us. Irenæus answered to the question of the Marcionites: What new thing did Jesus bring? with the words "*Omnem novitatem attulit semet ipsum afferens*"—"He brought all that was new, in bringing Himself."

PART II
THE COMMUNION OF PAUL WITH CHRIST

I

THE TASK, THE SOURCES AND THE METHOD.
PRELIMINARY EXEGETICAL QUESTIONS

IN these lectures we are to discuss Paul's communion with Christ. This I hold to be no small detail of his teaching, but the very centre of his religion. In saying this, I know that I am definitely contradicting certain investigators of Paulinism. I think especially of methods of investigation current on the Continent both in the past and at the present day. If I could ask you to look with me through the most important books on Paul that have lately been issued, you would probably discover the following:

1. Communion with Christ is practically never regarded as the central matter, but some attention is given to it as an occasional side-issue.

2. Other points of doctrine are taken as the centre of Pauline theology, for example, the

fight against the Law, the doctrine of Justification, or the doctrine of Redemption, or almost anything else.

In the nineteenth century investigation of Paul's teaching has had a strongly doctrinaire tendency. Paul has been thought of by scholars as the first great thinker and teacher, as the great theologian of primitive Christianity. The other Christian doctors, Athanasius, Anselm, Schleiermacher follow him, with differences certainly, but still on the whole in the same line; and the task of the modern theologian is, out of the scattered fragments of these thinkers, to discover their system, in the case of Paul to find Paulinism.

Neither this method of setting the question nor of answering it is valueless. Much that has been worked out is certainly of permanent value; and it would be not only lacking in respect, but also in gratitude, to fail to recognise this. But taken all together, I regard this method of investigation of Paulinism as mistaken, and this from four different standpoints:—

1. Paul is by this means transferred from

AND THE FAITH OF PAUL 155

his original sphere, from the sphere of vital religion, into the sphere of theology which, while it is not quite foreign to him, is obviously secondary. Instead we must try to understand him first in his primitive religious originality.

2. Paul is by this means—this is a generalisation from the first objection—transferred from the sphere of charismatic and intuitive simplicity into the sphere of reflection, which though not strange to him, is historically not his creative sphere.

3. By this means, Paul is torn out of the antique Oriental world, and transferred into the modern Occidental world.

4. By this means, Paul is removed, along with what he saw and bore witness to, from the capacity of simple men, such as he himself depicted in his own mission church in 1 Corinthians 1.

This last objection forms a very strong argument against the doctrinaire investigation of Paul. It is no less than grotesque to imagine the fantastic idea of reading to the Christians of Corinth, Thessalonica or Philippi in the time of Nero, a modern book on Paulinism in a vulgar Greek translation. Certain adepts of anthroposophy of to-day state that there is a secret " Akasha "-chronicle of all that has ever happened, and that they are able to read it. Sometimes, perhaps, they even go to the extent of making it a film of ghosts of the past, and so could even let us come into conversation with the poor saints of Paul's churches. I fear that if we read to these poor saints a book on Paulinism, we should bring them all into the condition of Eutychus of Troas, the one man who managed to sleep while Paul was speaking.

But humour apart, it must be emphasised in all earnestness that the whole Pauline missionary activity becomes a riddle, if it is supposed that Paul preached in the small cities and among the common people of Syria, Europe and Asia Minor in the way that his teaching is set forth in books on Paulinism.

We can contrast a parallel fact out of the history of modern thought. We have proofs of the sort of impression made by the doctrinaire portrait of Paul on foremost thinkers of

the nineteenth century. I mention Graf
Schack, Lagarde and Nietzsche. It is known
that these men, not only could by no means
understand Paul, but that they even rejected
him with the sharpest words and with strong
invectives. Nevertheless it was not the real
Paul that they rejected ; it was the unreal—
the Paulinism Paul, a Paul not to be found in
his own writings, but only in books about him.

Whoever is closely connected at the present
day with foreign missionary work must recognise as axiomatic that Paul, taking him altogether as a religious personality, cannot have
held complicated theological ideas. He must
have been simple. For, as a matter of fact,
by his evangelistic methods, he produced a
network of Christian churches in the Mediterranean world which formed the beginnings
of the great œcumenical organisation of the
Church. In his own life and afterwards, he
was not without success. The well-known,
witty saying of my venerable colleague, Adolf
von Harnack, that in the second century
after Christ only one man understood Paul—
Marcion—and that he misunderstood him (in

the last lecture I expect to investigate this point), is probably influenced by the difficulties raised by the doctrinaire picture of Paul. You could alter this saying of Harnack in this sense: that in the nineteenth century many people in the West thought they understood Paul, but everyone understood him differently, and many misunderstood him. Please do not take the definiteness of this statement as a piece of arrogance. I can assure you that I struggle against every form of arrogance in the field of scientific investigation. And here there is no mere alternative; it is not the question whether Paul was a prophet or a theologian; it is all a question of accent. On what, as we look at Paul, must we lay the accent? Is it to be on his religion, or on his theology? on his personal relationship to Christ, or on his Christology? The definiteness of the alternative is intended to vitalise the discussion.

What I am aiming at in these lectures will, I think, be clear from what I have said. I hope to show that Paul's religion has to be understood by means of his experience of

AND THE FAITH OF PAUL 159

communion with the living, exalted Christ. What I want to answer is this question: What is the moving energy which we meet whenever we come across Paul, even in the smallest details of his letters? May I try to answer by means of a simile? As when one travels on an ocean steamer, wherever one is, by day or night, on deck or below, one notices, whether softly or more strongly, the vibration from the working of the engines, and in the end one vibrates in unison with it : so to this great religious genius communion with Christ was the constant vibrating energy of life.

* * *

Where can we approach Paul? The question of the sources appears to be simple, and is so. Our sources are, of course, the letters of Paul. But we must seek to comprehend them as non-literary letters distinct from literary epistles.

The letters of Paul share with their writer the fate of having been frequently misjudged. Their intimate character, their soul, has been misunderstood. They have been regarded as pamphlets in letter form or at any rate as literary productions, as the theological works of the great apostolic thinker.

But these letters are not the products of literary art, but of actual life. They were the outcome of a definite situation, not to be repeated; they are "survivals" of Paul's missionary and pastoral endeavour. These letters are simply a substitute for spoken intercourse, and it is of great importance in their exegesis to imagine them as spoken (that is dictated) and to try to restore the modulation of the living and by no means bookish words. Each of Paul's letters is a portrait of Paul, and therein lies the unique value of Paul's letters as material for our task.

* **

The question, also, of the method of investigation is easily answered. We ought to read the letters of Paul as unliterary letters, not as literary epistles, not as carefully-thought-out pieces of a system that was being elaborated; we must read them as confessions, inspired by particular situations. It

AND THE FAITH OF PAUL 161

is not necessary for us to suppose that these separate special expressions can be, or were meant to be, combined into a systematic doctrine.

A special methodological rule, which appears to me to be important, is this : we find in most expressions of religious thought, that there is a tendency to the use of synonyms. The same idea is expressed in different words at different times. It is the chief task of a scientific reproduction of such teaching to demonstrate how like the sense is in these various expressions. One can thus characterise the differences between the doctrinaire method and the other method : the doctrinaire method has very little recognition of the synonymity of the various Pauline expressions. We could express this graphically. There are two possibilities of scientific reproduction. Both regard the whole of Paul's world of thought as a circle, and they mark out the single varieties of thought by the radii. The doctrinaire method sees the radii as thick lines ; the other method sees the circumference of the circle as a thick line.

When I come to speak of Justification, Reconciliation, Redemption and other similar thoughts, I shall have more to say about this contrast in method.

* * *

EXEGETICAL PRELIMINARIES

Before we come to the subject itself, I regard it as necessary to consider some preliminary questions of exegesis. There are especially certain linguistical problems. Like all creative men, Paul coined new expressions for himself. So I want to draw your attention to the following formulæ used by Paul: the formulæ "in Christ," "with Christ," through Christ"; the use of the genitive Ἰησοῦ Χριστοῦ ("of Jesus Christ"), the formulæ "in the blood of Christ," and "in the name of Christ." I believe all these expressions are fundamental for our understanding of the Pauline experience of communion with Christ. But the commentators have not explained them by any means in the same way. There are nothing less than enormous differences in the interpre-

AND THE FAITH OF PAUL

tation of these formulæ ; and yet one might even say that the understanding of Paul depended on the understanding of his prepositions.

I must remind you that we have, in our academic circles, different types of feeling for the Greek language. The older generation had a feeling for Greek regulated by classical Attic ; some of us have the feeling for Greek regulated by the popular Hellenistic Greek. I am glad to be able to say that in this we find British scholars standing in the first line ; most prominent stands my late dear friend, James Hope Moulton.

The position taken up with regard to the before-mentioned Pauline formulæ depends largely on the feeling for Greek language. About all these formulæ in the end one question is to be answered : Do the sentences refer to the exalted Christ, or to the so-called Jesus of History ? I do not think I am making a false statement when I say that most of the commentators maintain in most places that these formulæ refer to the historical Jesus. I beg you to test them, whether they must not apply, at least in most places, to the exalted Christ. We can, in German, very briefly express the differences between these two views. We contrast "*das Werk Christi*" and "*das Wirken Christi.*" That is to say, we contrast His work as something finished in the past, with His action as something still going on. So we can ask: Do these formulæ apply to the finished work of Christ, or to His continued action now?

In the first place, I want to say a word or two about the formula "in Christ."[1] The word "in"[2] seems to be most trifling. Anyone who knows nothing of biblical investigation will be surprised to hear that in the last thirty years more than a dozen larger or smaller monographs and articles have been written on this subject. Let me here add a personal recollection. As a young scholar, I investigated this formula "in Christ." My teacher, Dr. Georg Heinrici, had suggested

[1] ἐν Χριστῷ, etc.   [2] Greek ἐν.

AND THE FAITH OF PAUL 165

that I should investigate the subject of baptism. But I am glad that through investigating the question of baptism, I was led to deal with this quite small point. My work was much helped at that time by the fact that there was no possibility for me to use the Septuagint Concordance. That seems to be a paradox; but it is true: Hatch and Redpath in those days had not got as far as the preposition "ἐν," and in consequence I was driven to reading through the whole of the Septuagint for myself, with the special view of discovering the uses of "ἐν." I wonder whether it would have been possible for me to read the whole Old Testament in Greek otherwise. So the lack of Hatch and Redpath was of the greatest value for myself.

In this unique case, in order that you may see how international and interdenominational scholarship proceeds in such matters, I will give you the titles of the works that have been written on this subject.

A very important critic of my booklet on the New Testament formula "in Christ"

("*Die neutestamentliche Formel 'in Christo Jesu,'*" Marburg, 1892) [1] was my colleague the late Dr. Johannes Weiss, in a study called " Paulinische Probleme " (Number 2 : " Die Formel ἐν Χριστῷ ’Ιησοῦ ") in our theological Quarterly, *Theologische Studien und Kritiken,* 1896. Then a South German pastor, Wilhelm Karl, wrote a book, the title of which is extremely remarkable : *Beiträge zum Verständnis der soteriologischen Erfahrungen und Spekulationen des Apostels Paulus*, Strassburg, 1896 (" Contributions to the Understanding of the Soteriological Experiences and Speculations of the Apostle Paul "). In this title you may find both the influence of the old dogmatic method and the influence of a more psychological method of reproduction of Paul's religion. For example, the horrible word " soteriological " is a very characteristic one for that old dogmatic point of view. On the other hand, " experience " is characteristic for the psychological method.

Some years later a young scholar in Western

[1] The present publisher of this booklet is J. C. B. Mohr (Dr. Siebeck), Tübingen.

Switzerland, M. Lucien Delieutraz, published a University Thèse about the same problem (*De l'Importance de l'Expression ἐν Χριστῷ 'Ιησοῦ dans Saint-Paul*, Genève, 1899).

I am glad also to mention the observations of my venerable Berlin predecessor, the late Dr. Bernhard Weiss (Johannes' father) in *Theol. Studien und Kritiken*, 1911, p. 531 ff.

In the last ten years there have been many new studies. Lic. Traugott Schmidt, a dear Berlin pupil of mine and afterwards a Göttingen Privatdocent, who died for his country in the war, first wrote a dissertation, *Christus in uns—Wir in Christus* ("Christ in us—We in Christ"), Göttingen, 1913. His widow published his bigger work, *Der Leib Christi* (*Σῶμα Χριστοῦ*) ("The Body of Christ"), Leipzig, 1919.

In the *Neutestamentliche Studien für Georg Heinrici* ("New Testament Studies presented to Georg Heinrici"), Leipzig, 1914, the Berlin clergyman, Lic. Hans Böhlig, contributed a short essay "*Ἐν κυρίῳ*" ("In the Lord"), and Johannes Lundberg, a Swedish lecturer added in *Uppsala Universitets Årsskrift*, 1916, a paper called "Kristusmystiken hos Paulus" ("Paul's Christ Mysticism").

One of the most profound investigations I have seen was published by the Bonn professor, Dr. Hans Emil Weber, "Die Formel 'in Christo Jesu' und die paulinische Christusmystik" ("The formula 'in Christ Jesus,' and Paul's Christ Mysticism"), in *Neue Kirchliche Zeitschrift*, 1920. If you really wish to study the problem you must absolutely add to all the quoted books, including my own, Weber's research.

There is also a sharp criticism of my results delivered by my Danish colleague, Professor J. P. Bang: "Var Paulus Mystiker?" ("Was Paul a Mystic?"), in *Teologisk Tidsskrift*, 1920.

In the Academic Inaugural Address of the Utrecht Professor, Dr. A. M. Brouwer, "Paulus Mysticus?" ("Paul a Mystic?"), Utrecht, 1921, and in the book of the South German scholar, Rudolf Paulus, *Das Christusproblem der Gegenwart. Untersuchung über das Verhältnis von Idee und Geschichte* ("The Christ Problem. A Study in the Relation of

Idea and History "), Tübingen, 1922, we find very remarkable chapters on our problem.

There must be mentioned also a Spanish investigator, the Jesuit father J. M. Bover, who wrote last year a study, published in Barcelona: *La Unión Mística " en Cristo Jesús " según el Apóstol San Pablo* (" The Mystical Communion ' in Christ Jesus ' according to St. Paul the Apostle "), and some weeks ago I got the most recent investigation I know by my dear Norwegian colleague, Dr. Lyder Brun of Kristiania University, " Zur Formel ' in Christus Jesus ' im Brief des Paulus an die Philipper " (" Concerning the formula ' in Christ Jesus ' in the letter of Paul to the Philippians "), published in the first volume of the *Symbolae Arctoae*.

I am sorry indeed not to be able to give a full list of recent British and American researches about our problem. When mentioning W. Morgan, *The Religion and Theology of Paul*, Edinburgh, 1917, Part II, and H. A. A. Kennedy, *The Theology of the Epistles*, London, 1919, Chapter VI, I am sure that there are others which I ought to note here. It is sad to have to confess that I have not seen them. The former free and valuable intercourse of British and American scholarship with us has been interrupted by the political events of the last decade. But I am glad to say that there are many colleagues on both sides of the Channel, who are extremely anxious to bring that sad period of interruption to an end and to reunite their scientific forces in co-operation above all things in New Testament research; and there are few scholars who are more anxious for this than I am. So if anyone could add to my " In Christ " list the studies written in English during the last decade, I would be very grateful indeed. International and interdenominational investigation of the New Testament is a parallelogram of forces. And it cannot be denied that as long as the old co-operation between the English-speaking and the German-speaking investigators is not fully restored that parallelogram of forces is only a vain desire.

* * *

AND THE FAITH OF PAUL

"In Christ"—what does it mean? I think if we wish to gain a real understanding of Paul, we should begin with this formula, and we should regard it in its connection with the other one, "Christ in me."[1] There cannot be any doubt that "Christ in me" means the exalted Christ living in Paul. That is indeed a confession coming from the very depths of the soul. Corresponding with this is the other assurance, that Paul is "in Christ." Christ, the exalted Christ, is Spirit;[2] therefore He can live in Paul and Paul in Him. Just as the air of life which we breathe is "in" us and fills us, and yet we at the same time live and breathe "in" this air, so it is with Paul's fellowship with Christ: Christ in him, he in Christ. This formula "in Christ" is a thoroughly Pauline technical word and is meant vividly and mystically, as also is the analogous "Christ in me."

The formula "in Christ" (or "in the Lord" and so on) occurs one hundred and sixty-four times in Paul's letters; it is really the characteristic expression of his Christianity.

[1] Gal. 2. 20.   [2] 2 Cor. 3. 17.

It has been, in my opinion, very often and very greatly misunderstood by the commentators; they have rationalised it; they have ignored it; under their hands it often has become a mere scrap of parchment; they disguised its inner mystical energy, in very many cases applying it to the so-called historic Jesus and to His work, regarded as finished in the past, instead of applying the formula to the present exalted Lord and to His action still going on.

Though weakened in effect by exegesis, the formula " in Christ " must be conceived as the peculiarly Pauline expression of the Apostle's most intimate fellowship with the living spiritual Christ. We may understand the wonderfully plastic character of this expression better when we consider that there are in the Pauline letters a good number of contrasting formulæ, coined by the same Paul, to express the old spheres in which he had been before he came in Christ. For example, he was " in the Flesh " (Rom. 7. 5; 8. 8, 9); " in Sins " (1 Cor. 15. 17); " in Adam " (1 Cor. 15. 22); " in the Law " (Gal. 5. 4;

Rom. 3. 19; 2. 12); "in the World" (Eph. 2. 12); "in Sufferings" (2 Cor. 6. 4). Now, he is "in Christ."

Regarding the extraordinary importance of this formula "in Christ," I ask you yourself to consider the question of interpretation. You will find a very good, a model example, in Rom. 3. 24: "being justified freely by his grace through the redemption that is in Christ Jesus."[1] No doubt, one of the greatest religious confessions of Paul, even of Christianity, even of mankind. How should we understand it?

In our German Bible, the Luther-Bible, we find the following translation, or rather interpretation, of the last line: "durch die Erlösung, so durch Christum Jesum geschehen ist," that is, "through the redemption that has been through Christ Jesus." You see, here the formula "in Christ" is identified with "through Christ" and the "redemption through Christ" is thought of as a matter of fact finished in the past.

[1] δικαιούμενοι δωρεὰν τῇ αὐτοῦ χάριτι διὰ τῆς ἀπολυτρώσεως τῆς ἐν Χριστῷ Ἰησοῦ.

Let us now compare the English Versions. I am very much obliged to the Warden of Woodbrooke for kindly lending me his fine copy of the English Hexapla (London, 1841). There is a wonderful harmony in the six old texts: Wiclif, Tyndale, Cranmer, the Geneva and the Rheims Bibles, and the Authorised too, all translate: "that *is in* Christ Jesus." The Revised Version has not altered this translation at all. And it was well done not to alter it. For this translation, so far as I can see, is the only possible and correct one. I doubt whether Dr. Moffatt's translation, "through the ransom provided in Christ Jesus," can be considered a better one. The English translation seems to be a good equivalent of the Greek text. It places no obstacle in the way of understanding Paul's confession as he understood it himself.

May I add, that there is in the Pauline letters a remarkable correspondence between the formula "in Christ" and the formula "in the (Holy) Spirit." The formula "in the Spirit," which occurs only nineteen times in Paul, is connected in nearly all these passages with the same characteristically Pauline fundamental notions, as the formula " in Christ." For example : faith, righteousness, justification, love, peace, sanctification—all these things Paul sees and experiences " in Christ " and also " in the Spirit " ; that means in fact: " in Christ who is the Spirit." [1] And in the same way the technical expressions " fellowship of the Son of God " [2] and " fellowship of the Holy Spirit " [3] are parallel, for the same experience is meant in both cases.

If you should ask me, whether there were before Paul analogies in religious thought and language, I would answer that, in my opinion, some Septuagint formulæ have influenced Paul when he coined his confession " in Christ."

* * *

There is another Pauline formula " with Christ " [4] which occurs, if I am right, five times in Paul's letters ; [5] the small number of the passages is not surprising. The greatest

[1] 2 Cor. 3. 17 : ὁ δὲ κύριος τὸ πνεῦμά ἐστιν.
[2] 1 Cor. 1. 9.   [3] 2 Cor. 13. 13 ; Phil. 2. 1.   [4] σὺν Χριστῷ.
[5] The passages are : 1 Thess. 4. 17 and 5. 10 ; 2 Cor. 13. 4 ; Phil. 1. 23 ; Rom. 8. 32.

176 THE RELIGION OF JESUS

specialist in the use of Greek prepositions, the late Dr. Tycho Mommsen, the brother of Theodor Mommsen, has shown that the Greek preposition σύν is an " aristocratic " one and therefore not very common at all.

This formula " with Christ " notes the higher stage of " in Christ." To be " in Christ " can be experienced here on earth. But he who is united " with Christ " is " face to face " with him,[1] he will have put off all that is fleshly and will possess a " spiritual body " similar to the body of Christ Himself. So the formula " with Christ " seems to be the eschatological expression, exactly as " in Christ " is the mystical one.

* * *

We find a third problem, and an important one, in the Pauline formula " through Christ."[2] How often do we hear it, and how often do we read it and use it, for example, in the end of our prayers! But in many cases, even when quoting Scripture passages, we do not consider what this " through Christ " really

[1] I Cor. 13. 12 : πρόσωπον πρὸς πρόσωπον.
[2] διὰ Χριστοῦ.

AND THE FAITH OF PAUL 177

means. There is a good investigation by Adolph Schettler, "*Die paulinische Formel 'Durch Christus'*" ("The Pauline Formula 'through Christ'"), Tübingen, 1907, and it seems to me he is right in emphasising that this formula "through Christ" in by far the greatest number of cases is also to be referred to the exalted spiritual Christ.

* * *

Fourthly, Paul's use of the genitive "of Jesus Christ"[1] is altogether very peculiar. There are a number of passages in the Pauline letters in which the ordinary grammatical scheme of "subjective genitive" and "objective genitive" proves insufficient. It is possible and in many cases necessary, in my opinion, to establish in Paul a peculiar type of genitive, say "genitivus communionis," a "mystic genitive," because it expresses the mystic communion.[2] This genitive "of Jesus

[1] Ἰησοῦ Χριστοῦ.

[2] For further details compare a forthcoming study of Dr. Otto Schmitz (University of Münster in Westfalen) which he is going to publish in the next part of his *Paulusstudien* (C. Bertelsmann, Gütersloh).

Christ" is here in the main identical with "in Christ." For example: the "faith of Jesus Christ" is really the "faith in Christ," that is faith is something which is effected in the vital union with the spiritual Christ. Note please the passages and compare for yourself the use of "faith of Jesus Christ,"[1] and of "faith in Christ Jesus."[2]

So we could note also other similar expressions: "the love of Christ," the "hope of Christ," the "patience of Christ," and many others; perhaps the most characteristic are the expressions "the sufferings of Christ"[3] and "the afflictions of Christ."[4]

* * *

There are two preliminaries still: what is the meaning of the Pauline formulæ "in the blood of Christ" and "in the name of Christ"?

It seems to me that the term "blood," in

[1] πίστις Ἰησοῦ Χριστοῦ, Gal. 2. 16; 2. 20; 3. 22; Eph. 3. 12; Phil. 3. 9; Rom. 3. 22; 3. 26.
[2] πίστις ἐν Χριστῷ Ἰησοῦ, Gal. 3. 26; 5. 6; Col. 1. 4; 2. 5; Eph. 1. 15; 1 Tim. 1. 14; 3. 13; 2 Tim. 1. 13; 3. 15.
[3] τὰ παθήματα τοῦ Χριστοῦ, 2. Cor. 1. 5; Phil. 3. 10.
[4] αἱ θλίψεις τοῦ Χριστοῦ, Col. 1. 24.

some cases at least, does not refer to the physical blood, once shed at the historic martyrdom. It is rather a vivid way of realising the Living One [1] who is also the Crucified and with whom Paul lives in mystic spiritual "fellowship of blood." This extremely remarkable expression alone, "fellowship of blood," [2] would be sufficient for the thesis, that there exists in the Pauline letters a mystic meaning of the word "blood," and I suppose that in the following passages we should prefer to paraphrase "in the blood of Christ" [3] by, "in the fellowship of the blood of Christ": Rom. 3. 25 (compare Eph. 1. 9); Rom. 5. 9 (compare Rom. 5. 10); Eph. 2. 13.

Finally, I think that also the often-discussed formula "in the name of our Lord Jesus Christ," [4] and so the formula "through

---

[1] Compare the interesting book of Dr. Otto Schmitz, *Die Opferanschauung des späteren Judentums und die Opferaussagen des Neuen Testamentes* ("The Conception of Sacrifice in later Judaism and the New Testament Ideas of Sacrifice"), Tübingen, 1910, p. 214 ff.

[2] κοινωνία τοῦ αἵματος τοῦ Χριστοῦ, 1 Cor. 10. 16.

[3] ἐν τῷ αἵματι τοῦ Χριστοῦ.

[4] ἐν τῷ ὀνόματα τοῦ κυρίου ἡμῶν Ἰησοῦ Χριστοῦ.

the name of our Lord Jesus Christ "[1] will receive fresh light when we consider it also as a technical expression of Paul's mystic language, as one of the many plastic terms coined or adopted by this deep religious personality to express the inner experiences of his communion with Christ.

* * *

In reviewing these exegetical preliminaries, I may say that I do not wish to compel you to accept any results in advance, but merely to show you the sort of problem with which we have to deal. There are two great possibilities: the first is this, that one interprets these formulæ and Paul himself more dogmatically by applying them to the finished work of Christ; or that we grasp them and Paul himself in a more mystical sense, by finding in them confessions of the action of the exalted Christ as a living power.

[1] διὰ τοῦ ὀνόματος τοῦ κυρίου ἡμῶν Ἰησοῦ Χριστοῦ.

II

THE BEGINNING AND ESSENTIAL NATURE OF COMMUNION WITH CHRIST

THE beginning of Paul's Communion with Christ is Damascus. Concerning this event, which no pagan historian took notice of, though in its results it was of world-wide importance, we possess two sources: the hints of the apostle himself, and three sketches in the Acts of the Apostles. These sketches, given in Acts 9., 22. and 26. are not in all details completely reconcilable with one another; but it seems to be certain from the nature of the case that they must be somehow derived from private confidential accounts given by Paul himself.

There might be also an indirect possibility for a better understanding of the Damascus episode. We might call to our aid the numerous analogies to the incident of conversion which the history of religion affords, especially the history of Christianity itself. But even if we should have a complete insight into the most important conversion stories of all centuries, we should never succeed in unravelling and analysing Paul's experience at Damascus without any residue of the inexplicable. What we can do is this: we can state with great certainty how Paul himself conceived of the incident.

There is a wonderful variety of expressions when he is speaking about it. He describes it with the technical expression for the epiphanies, the appearances of the Divinity, used by the Septuagint, and used by himself before when mentioning the appearances of Christ to the other Apostles: " He appeared to me also." [1] It was the living Christ who appeared, and Paul hints that the Damascus Manifestation of Christ to him was the last in the series.

Another time, he says, with still more of ancient popular vividness, " I have seen Jesus

[1] 1 Cor. 15. 8, ὤφθη κἀμοί.

AND THE FAITH OF PAUL 183

our Lord."[1] It seems to me also that the well-known saying, "I was apprehended by Christ Jesus," is a confession concerning the Damascus experience.[2] And he says in more general terms: "the mystery of Christ was made known to me by revelation."[3] But there is another confession which, I think, is the most interesting one, because Paul speaks of his experience almost as a modern psychologist would: "it was the good pleasure of God . . . to reveal His Son *in me.*"[4] Please note this "in me"; there is a close connection between this Pauline term and another one I have to mention immediately. In Paul's memory of what happened near Damascus there was always—as he himself hints[5]—the impression of a great blaze of light comparable to God's first shining day that broke forth out of the darkness at the

[1] 1 Cor. 9. 1, Ἰησοῦν τὸν κύριον ἡμῶν ἑόρακα.
[2] Phil. 3. 12, κατελήμφθην ὑπὸ Χριστοῦ Ἰησοῦ. Καταλαμβάνειν = to apprehend, is in my opinion a technical mystical expression.
[3] Eph. 3. 3, κατὰ ἀποκάλυψιν ἐγνωρίσθη μοι τὸ μυστήριον.
[4] Gal. 1. 15, 16, ἀποκαλύψαι τὸν υἱὸν αὐτοῦ ἐν ἐμοί.
[5] 2 Cor. 4. 6.

creation. So, too, in those sketches given by Luke in the Acts the Damascus Christophany is painted with the universal colours of antiquity, in the magnificent flood of light always employed to represent manifestations of the divine.

Combining all these observations, we can say: an experience which Paul looks upon as caused by God, which betokens to him with absolute certainty that the living Christ has been revealed to him, or that Paul himself has been taken possession of by Christ, and which includes also the inward transformation and at the same time apostolic commission of the man who hitherto had been a persecutor, —all this the Damascus Christophany was to Paul himself. I think this description of his own impressions concerning the incident of his conversion is sufficient for the historian. But there is one experience of the convert which adds another important fact concerning the conversion. When Paul describes his position as a Christian by saying, "Christ liveth *in me*," [1] he himself gives fresh light on

[1] Gal. 2. 20, ζῇ δὲ ἐν ἐμοὶ Χριστός.

the phrase, "it was the good pleasure of God . . . to reveal His Son *in me.*"[1] For Paul himself Damascus was the very beginning of the indwelling of Christ.

We must therefore not isolate the Damascus experience, but regard it as the foundation occurrence in mysticism, as the inaugurating mystical experience of this religious genius.

The first Damascus revelation certainly meant for Paul the direct attainment of a pinnacle of spiritual experience, and we may take it for granted that his normal experience of communion with Christ moved on a more temperate plane of spiritual life. From time to time, and even considerably later, Paul experienced other peaks of spiritual life, hours of passionate, intensified intercourse with the living Lord. I refer you here to the classical words of 2 Corinthians 12. 1–10. In this passage I consider the hints about his thrice-repeated prayer to Christ as more important than those about being taken up into the third Heaven.

The conversion of the persecutor to the

[1] Gal. 1. 16.

follower and of the apostle of the Pharisees to the apostle of Christ was a sudden one. But it was no magical transformation, it was psychologically prepared for, both negatively and positively. Negatively, by the experiences which the soul of the young Pharisee, in its passionate hunger for righteouness, had had under the yoke of the Law. We hear the echo of his groanings even twenty or thirty years afterwards in the letters of the convert. Like a curse there had come upon him the awful discovery that even for the most earnest conscience, it is impossible really to keep the whole Law. Positively the conversion was no doubt prepared for on the one hand by the prophetic inwardness of the old revelation acting upon Paul the Jew, whom we ought to consider as a mystic before Damascus. On the other hand by a relatively close familiarity with the genuine tradition about Jesus and the effects that Jesus was able to produce in the persons of His confessors whom Paul persecuted. I do not think it probable that the young zealot was ever personally acquainted with the earthly Jesus, although weighty voices have again declared recently in favour of this hypothesis. The saying "We have known Christ after the flesh"[1] must be understood, in my opinion, thus: "I have known him before in a fleshly method," "I have not had a real spiritual understanding of Him." It does not mean: "I have known before the earthly Jesus personally"; for if we would refer the words to personal acquaintance with the historical Jesus, the following conclusion, "now we know Him no more," would be trivial.

Paul knew the historical Jesus only so far as the Lord continued to live in His sayings and in His disciples.

Thus the lightning of Damascus strikes no empty void, but finds plenty of inflammable material in the soul of the young mystic. We see the flames shoot up, and we feel that the glow then kindled has lost none of its force a generation later in the man grown aged: Christ is in Paul, Paul is in Christ.

With these words we have not only grasped the secret of the beginning and essential

[1] 2 Cor. 5. 16, ἐγνώκαμεν κατὰ σάρκα Χριστόν.

nature of Paul's communion with Christ, the secret of all Paul's religion—we have also described it in terms made sacred by the apostle : Christ in Paul, Paul in Christ.[1]

It is, no doubt, generally admitted that Paul's religion centred in Christ. But how differently the theological schools conceive of the Christ-centred Christianity of Paul! Often it has been represented as identical with Christology. But Paul's religion is Christ-centred in a far deeper and far more realistic sense, it is not first of all a doctrine concerning Christ, it is communion with Christ, it is fellowship with Christ. Paul lives " in Christ "—that is, in the living and present spiritual Christ who is about on all sides, dwells in Him, speaks to Him, speaks in Him, and through Him.[2] To Paul Christ is not a person of the past, with whom he can have intercourse only by meditating on His words as they have been handed down. To Paul Christ is not a great " historic " figure, but a

[1] Compare Gal. 2. 20 and other passages, and then all those numerous " in Christ " passages of the Pauline letters.

[2] Gal. 2. 20 ; 2 Cor. 12. 9 ; 2 Cor. 13. 3.

AND THE FAITH OF PAUL 189

reality and power of the present, an " energy " whose life-giving power is daily made perfect in him. It is a most remarkable fact that the term " energy," so familiar with us to-day, is a characteristic Pauline technical expression.[1]

In Greek we can make the contrast between these different conceptions very clear indeed by saying that Paul is not so much the great *Christologos* as the great *Christophoros*,[2] not so much the great thinker in Christology as the great bearer of Christ. It is very fruitful to consider this difference between *Christologos* and *Christophoros*, and I venture to mention a short paper of mine about it, written some time ago under the title " Tragende und stählende Kräfte des Neuen Testaments " (" Bearing and Strengthening Powers of the New Testament ") in a Festschrift (a book in honour) for my venerable Berlin colleague Julius Kaftan, Tübingen, 1920.

* * *

If now we ask : what was Paul's conception of the Spiritual Christ ? it is best to start from

[1] Compare Phil. 2. 21 ; Col. 2. 29 ; Eph. 1. 19.
[2] Χριστολόγος, Χριστοφόρος.

the sharp contrast in which the *pneuma* (spirit) always stands to the *sarx* (flesh). The spiritual Christ has indeed a *soma* (body), but it is a spiritual [1] (that is " heavenly ") body [2] consisting of divine effulgence. Sharp philosophically pointed definition of the concept " spiritual " there is happily none in Paul. The Apostle remains popular and, in true ancient style, vivid in his formulation. He probably thought of some light ethereal form of existence, such as he doubtless attributed also to God. But there is no binding definition. We have the greatest possible latitude if we wish to transplant the Apostle's ideas concerning Christ into our own religious thought. If Paul had given a definition he would have defined as a man of the ancient world, in a manner more realistic, more massive and more concrete than a modern thinker, but certainly not materialistically.

What Paul formally newly created or rather introduced into the mysticism of Christ, was not definitions, but an abundant store of technical phrases expressing often in

[1] 1 Cor. 15. 45 ff.   [2] 1 Cor. 15. 47 ff.

popular language the spiritual fellowship between Christ and His own. First of all that wonderful term " fellowship " (communion),[1] and then many others, especially those formulæ already mentioned in the first lecture.

The question : " What, according to Paul, brings about communion with Christ ? " is answered from the hints which we have given concerning Paul's conversion. It is *God* who brings about fellowship with Christ.[2] God is always the acting power, man is reacting. Not that every Christian had an experience equal to that of Paul on the road to Damascus, but everyone who has communion with Christ has received this gift of the Spirit from God Himself. Baptism does not bring about, but only sets the seal to the fellowship of Christ. The Lord's Supper does not bring about the fellowship ; it only brings it into prominence. In every case it is God's grace that is decisive. Paul's Christians can say with him : By the grace of God I am what I am.[3]

[1] Greek κοινωνία.
[2] 1 Cor. 1. 9, 30 ; 2 Cor. 1. 21 ff. ; 4. 6.
[3] 1 Cor. 15. 10.

I have already mentioned that it is very probable that Paul was a mystic before Damascus. So I think there were, besides this mystical predisposition, not wanting influences, chiefly coming from the Septuagint, that acted upon him as stimuli. In the Greek Old Testament there are a considerable number of prominent passages—and here an important Hellenisation of the original is revealed—in which the formulæ " in God " and " in the Lord " are used in a mystical sense.

There is a well-known parallel to this supposed pre-Christian Jewish mysticism: Philo, who was not only a Platonic thinker, but even a Platonic mystic too, interpreted Septuagint religion in a mystical way. We possess an enormous mass of Philonic mystical lines. Concerning the pre-Christian mystic Paul we hear only the last low sounds of an almost forgotten prelude to his own jubilate " Rejoice in the Lord," [1] when we find in Septuagint, " Yet I will exult in the Lord." [2]

[1] Phil. 3. 1; 4. 4.
[2] Habakkuk, 3. 18, ἐγὼ δὲ ἐν τῷ κυρίῳ ἀγαλλιάσομαι.

There is only one line, but it is a very jewel, which shows us the pre-Christian mystic Paul in a close connection with Greek mysticism: that confession in the speech on the Mars' Hill: " In Him [that is, in God] we live, and move, and have our being." [1]

" In Him," " In God "—this pre-Christian mystical confession, which is especially frequent in the Septuagint Psalms, is a great favourite with Paul. Paul the Christian's rallying-cry " in Christ " is the more vivid substitute for the old sacred formula, and places the piety of Paul in the great coherent body of mysticism in general: Paul's Christianity is Christ mysticism.

* * *

Here we must turn aside to consider an important problem. I have used the word " mysticism," and thereby have introduced a problematic idea which must be considered. When we speak in Germany of mysticism everyone present, generally speaking, has a different idea of what one means,

[1] Acts 17. 28, ἐν αὐτῷ γὰρ ζῶμεν καὶ κινούμεθα καὶ ἐσμέν.

and the discussion therefore is often characterised by a tendency to talk at cross purposes. I suppose that in other countries the same thing happens.

To express the matter quite clearly, the chief distinction is this : some use the word mysticism in a good sense, others in a bad sense ; some have a favourable view of mysticism, others have an unfavourable view. For this reason, I would like to draw attention to a remarkable linguistic fact. In German we understand the word " Mysticismus " altogether in the evil sense ; we are accustomed to say " Mystik " when we mean it in a good sense. I therefore have always to overcome a certain aversion due to my native method of speaking, when in speaking in English, I use the word " mysticism " in a good sense.

In endless debates with my students in Heidelberg and Berlin, with my colleagues and with preachers in conferences and at holiday courses, it has become clear to me that it is most essential to distinguish two chief types of mysticism. In both cases, what is under discussion is a personal communion of the individual with God, direct intercourse with God. This directness of intercourse with the Deity seems to me to be the essential thing in every kind of mysticism. Between God and man there is here no intervention of doctrinaire hair-splitting, no system of objective salvation and of salvation subjectively appropriated, no apparatus of rites, no bridge of priesthood and saints. Instead of that, there exists an immediate contact, an " I " speaks to a " thou," unites with Him : in Him lives, moves, and has its being. That is the general description of what we call mysticism.

Now there are two main types which seem to me to be distinguished from one another. The one type is everywhere present where the mystic regards his communion with God as an experience in which the action of God upon him produces a reaction towards God. The other type of mysticism is that in which the mystic regards his communion with God as his own action, from which a reaction follows on the part of Deity.

The token by which the distinction can be recognised is this: has the action of God, or the action of man, the priority? The one type is the mystic who reacts in response to the action of God. The other type is the mystic who, by his own action, endeavours to produce the divine reaction. In the end, the whole difference is equivalent to the contrast between the religion of grace and the religion of works. All depends on who has the initiative, whether God or man: and on this basis I distinguish between Reacting Mysticism and Acting Mysticism. Allow me, therefore, to use these rather unusual expressions as technical terms.

I am not unaware that there are also mixed forms; for example, if we asked the greater representatives of acting mysticism they would often answer that the psychological starting-point of their action has been the consciousness of the action of God. But I do not think it is necessary here to enter upon the extraordinarily interesting problem of the mixed forms of mysticism. If we desire to become clear about the Pauline mysticism, it is enough for us to keep these two types sharply distinguished.

Most of those who talk about mysticism have the second type in mind—the acting mysticism. It stands well in the front of the religious history of all people and all times. In primitive religion it took up thoroughly crude and coarsely sensual forms. In higher religions it became sublimated and combined itself with philosophical systems. It has become a great power of the first magnitude in all civilised religious systems.

In the higher forms it is characterised by definite kinds of mystical action. This action is thought of as a means of ascent of the soul to God, or as a means of entrance of the soul into God. This mystical method early learnt to give up hope of outward methods of stimulation, such as fasting, the use of narcotics, the rhythmic motion of sacred dances, or the magic of the holy place. Instead of these, it developed a system of spiritual exercises. These spiritual exercises, in a highly developed and most refined art of training of the soul, cut for the mystic the steps in the rock of surrounding reality, upon which he, step by step, goes on to a complete unity with the Deity. There seems to me a clear connection between the methods used by mystics of different bodies, for example, between those employed by the Jesuits in educating souls and those of the newest anthroposophical school.

There frequently exists among these mystics who are driven by the ego, a trace of desire for merely egotistical enjoyment; *fruitio Dei*, enjoyment of God is the goal. To get rid of the world, its torment, its sin, but also its duties and its work, to flutter into the eternal light, to dip into the sea of eternity. This mysticism is not terrified even by Titanic daring: deification is its final desire.

In theological debates, those who talk about mysticism mostly think of this second type, of the acting type which longs for the enjoyment of absorption in the Deity. This type of acting mysticism has impressed the general mind more by its caricature than by its nobler, weightier representatives. So it is quite possible that the sentence " Paul was a mystic " might be misunderstood to mean " Paul was a howling dervish."

On the other hand, I want now to point out that to me Paul appears to be a classical type of the reacting mystic, and that it is only another expression of this fact if I pronounce the general sentence that the Pauline religion is the religion of grace. The proof that Paul is a reacting mystic will be given in these lectures themselves. In particular we shall, in the last lecture, unfold the great problem, of the relation between the Pauline mysticism and the Pauline ethic. We shall have to inquire whether in Pauline mysticism there are forces present that weaken the ethos, or forces that strengthen the ethos.

It will perhaps make for the better understanding of the whole series of lectures if I say at once : Paul himself knew the difference between the two types of mysticism, the reacting and the acting type. And more than this, he waged a severe battle against the acting mysticism, and definitely stated the purity and power of the reacting mysticism. I think that his polemic against the inspired people in Corinth as he displays it to us in plastic dramatic form in 1 Corinthians, was in the end a polemic against the acting mysticism, or at the very least against one of the mixed forms of mysticism, about which I have already spoken. It is true that an act of God, the gift of the Holy Spirit, lay behind all the mysticism of the spirituals in Corinth, but on the whole these people give one the impression of being acting mystics. We might apply to this group-drunkenness of ecstasy of enjoyment among the inspired people in Corinth the word of Goethe:

"So jag' ich von Begierde zu Genuss
Und im Genuss verschmacht' ich vor Begierde"

"I hurry from desire to enjoyment, and in the midst of enjoyment, I languish for the desire." All that Paul says about this ecstatic chaos in really creative words of well-considered warning, soberness and moderation, seem to be the words of a man who did not act from himself but who reacted to divine grace.

III

SALVATION IN COMMUNION WITH CHRIST

CHRIST the Living One, highly exalted with the Father, but also by God's grace as Spirit living in Paul and Paul in Him—that is the Apostle's assurance of Christ and experience of Christ. There is no dualism in Paul of the transcendence and immanence of Christ. We see rather two moods of his piety both of which could exist side by side in his capacious soul and the polarity of which gives to the inner life of the Apostle its prophetic tension.

There is no doubt that the assurance of Damascus, " Christ in me," with the corresponding assurance " I in Christ," is the really creative power for his religious thought and religious language. These mystic experiences have concentrated in the deep and sensitive soul of the convert an inexhaustible religious energy. In all directions Paul now radiates this energy, which he calls "the power of Christ,"[1] and dispenses "the riches of Christ,"[2] or "the blessing of Christ,"[3] or "the fullness of Christ,"[4] which have accrued to him.

All these Pauline terms, "power of Christ," "riches of Christ," "blessing of Christ," "fullness of Christ," are very characteristic. It seems to me that the type of thought they represent is not dogmatical but poetical; and they are synonym expressions of one and the same religious experience. Therefore we must not isolate them, and we must not dogmatise them. Paul did not coin them for the Universities of the nineteenth or twentieth centuries. If he had written his letters for future generations he would not have coined these wonderful expressions for Anselm or Johann Gerhard, but for Johann Sebastian Bach.

But there is also one well-known technical religious term which is a short and comprehensive expression for all that streamed

[1] 2 Cor. 12. 9, ἡ δύναμις τοῦ Χριστοῦ. Cf. 1 Cor. 5.
[2] Eph. 3. 8, τὸ πλοῦτος τοῦ Χριστοῦ. Cf. Eph. 2. 7.
[3] Rom. 15. 29. εὐλογία Χριστοῦ.
[4] Eph. 4. 13, τὸ πλήρωμα τοῦ Χριστοῦ.

AND THE FAITH OF PAUL

through him and took effect from him: the Greek word *pistis*, which we are accustomed to translate as "faith."

It is true, *pistis* (faith) is one of the most frequently discussed Pauline conceptions, but I think we can formulate the Apostle's faith even more precisely than it usually is formulated.

Speaking about this question I must make a preliminary remark, namely: It is not very easy to express my opinion about *pistis* (faith) in English, because this requires a discussion about the Pauline use of the preposition ἐν ("in"). In the German Bible this preposition is translated either *an* or *in;* in the English Bible it is translated in most cases literally *in*. So I think the expression "faith in Christ" is very common with you. But I wonder whether "faith in Christ" is understood by you always in the Pauline sense, namely with special stress on the preposition, with accent on the "in." I am very much obliged to my dear friend and translator Mr. Lionel R. M. Strachan, now of Birmingham University, that, in his excellent translation of my book about St. Paul, he made important allusion to this point. There he says that many interpreters defined that Pauline term as "faith in Christ" with no special stress on the preposition, so that the phrase is equivalent to "believing in" or, in the archaic language of the English Bible, "believing on Christ" (as we say in German, "Glaube an Christus"). Mr. Strachan adds that, in English, we might therefore conceivably employ, as Carlyle would have done, a hyphen between "in" and the preceding word.

Again the not infrequent genitival combination, which I mentioned in the first lecture, "faith of Christ Jesus"[1] has very often been identified with "believing *on* Christ," and so also the prepositional phrases "*faith in Christ Jesus*,"[2] "*to believe in Christ*,"[3] and "*the faithful in Christ*."[4]

---

[1] πίστις Χριστοῦ 'Ιησοῦ. See Gal. 2. 16, 20; 3. 22; Eph. 3. 12; Phil. 3. 9; Rom. 3. 22, 26.

[2] πίστις ἐν Χριστῷ 'Ιησοῦ. Gal. 3. 26; 5. 6; Col. 1. 4; 2. 5 (εἰς); Eph. 1. 15 (ἐν τῷ κυρίῳ 'Ιησοῦ); 1 Tim. 1. 14; 3. 13; 2 Tim. 1. 13; 3. 15.

[3] πιστεύειν εἰς Χριστὸν 'Ιησοῦν, Gal. 2. 16; Phil. 1. 29; Eph. 1. 13 (ἐν).

[4] πιστοὶ ἐν Χριστῷ 'Ιησοῦ, Eph. 1. 1; Col. 1. 2.

AND THE FAITH OF PAUL 205

Let me insert here, please, an observation concerning the English translations. I find that in Rom. 3. 22 the Authorised Version translates "*by faith of Jesus Christ*," the Revised translates "*through faith in Jesus Christ*," adding in the margin as alternative " or, *of*." I think the Authorised is the better one in this case too, although " faith *in* Jesus Christ " if being understood with special stress on the " in " is a correct rendering of the Pauline idea.

What, then, is " faith in Christ " and " faith of Christ " in Pauline thought ? May I answer firstly negatively : " faith of Jesus Christ " according to Paul, is not the faith which the so-called historical Jesus Himself had, though some liberal theologians of our age have adopted this interpretation. We find this use of a subjective genitive after *pistis* (faith) in the well-known Pauline formula " faith of Abraham."[1] The " faith of Abraham " is the faith which Abraham in the sacred past had held, that is to say unconditional trust in the living God in spite

[1] πίστις 'Αβραάμ, Rom. 4. 12, 16.

of all temptations to doubt, a faith heroic by its " Nevertheless ! "

" Faith of Jesus Christ," however, seems to me to be the same as " faith in Christ "—that is : the faith which lives in Paul in the fellowship with the spiritual Christ. I may remind you here of the observations made in the first lecture about that mystical use of the genitive *Ἰησοῦ Χριστοῦ* in Paul's religious language. This faith of Paul in fellowship with Christ, in communion with Christ is faith in God,[1] faith in God identical with the faith of Abraham. The " faith of Abraham " was, according to Paul, the normal and ideal faith; Law made it impossible afterwards, but it is now again possible to us and effectual in communion with Christ. Separated from Christ, Paul says we are *in the cosmos* (in the world) without God,[2] in union with Christ we have boldness to approach God.[3]

Paul's faith, therefore, is union with God, which is brought about in fellowship with

---

[1] Paul uses the preposition *ἐπί* for this faith in God in Rom. 4. 5, 24; 9. 33; 10. 11.
[2] Eph. 2. 12.   [3] Eph. 3. 12.

Christ, and which is like that of Abraham, an unshakable confidence in the grace of God.

* * *

Now we must try to recognise the Apostle's "faith of Christ" as the centre of energy from which radiate all his confessions concerning salvation in Christ. Here, I think, lies the most important problem for the student of Pauline religion. Its solution lies in perceiving that the various Pauline testimonies about salvation are refractions of the one single ray, the faith of Christ, that all these confessions are psychically synonymous.

Concerning this methodological point of view, I may remind you of the hints given in the first lecture about the synonymy of the religious terms of Paul. An older method isolated the so-called "concepts" of justification, reconciliation, forgiveness, redemption, adoption, and then reconstructed from these isolated, and thereby dogmatised, "concepts," the "system" of "Paulinism," a very geometrical system indeed.

When we have, however, recognised the

synonymy of Pauline religious confessions we see many rays streaming in all directions from the one point of light given in the experience of communion with Christ.

There are many other synonyms besides, but the following are the most important: justification, reconciliation, forgiveness, redemption and adoption.

In all these figurative expressions man stands before God each time in a different guise before the same God, first as an accused person, secondly as an enemy, thirdly as a debtor, fourthly and fifthly as a slave. In all these cases man is in an abnormal and bad position. Then, in Christ, he comes into the normal and good position.

As an *accused person* [1] man stands before God's judgment seat. This is part of the mighty complex of religious imagery which surrounds the fundamental word "justification," and which has its psychological starting-point in the old Jewish and old apostolic expectation of the last judgment. In Christ the accused becomes "unaccused"; [2]

[1] Rom. 8. 33. [2] 1 Cor. 1. 8; Col. 1. 22, ἀνεγκλήτους.

he is awarded not condemnation[1] but liberty.[2]

" Acquittal "—that is the meaning of St. Paul's " justification "[3]; and the acquittal experienced " in Christ " coincides with justification " out of faith,"[4] or " through faith,"[5] because faith is, as we saw, union with Christ.

Paul's justification " out of " faith or " through " faith has often been misunderstood, and is still often misunderstood by vulgar Protestantism at the present day, in something like this form: justification is reckoned as the reward given by God to man for his performance of faith Paul himself perhaps, especially in the fourth chapter of Romans,[6] gave occasion to this misunderstanding by the emphatic use which he made of a text from the Septuagint concerning the faith of Abraham. The phrasing of this

[1] Rom. 8. 1, κατάκριμα.   [2] Rom. 8. 2, ἠλευθέρωσεν.
[3] Gal. 2. 17; 2 Cor. 5. 21; Rom. 3. 24; 8. 33; Phil. 3. 9.
[4] Greek ἐκ generally translated " by," or " of," Gal. 2. 16; 3. 8, 24; 5. 5; Rom. 3. 26, 30; 5. 1; 9. 30; 10. 6.
[5] Greek διά, Gal. 2. 16; Rom. 3. 22, 25, 28 (variant), 30.
[6] Rom. 4. 3 f., 9 f., 22 ff.; cf. also Gal. 3. 6.

quotation,[1] " His faith was reckoned," [2] lends support to the mechanical interpretation just mentioned.

But we must not isolate this passage, and on no account may we look upon " reckon " as the characteristic word to use in connection with justification. Paul employs the word " reckon " under the compulsion of the terms of his quotation. When due regard is paid to the whole of his utterances concerning faith and righteousness, then it must be said : faith according to Paul is not a human performance before God, but a divine influence upon man in Christ. To use those technical terms given in Lecture II, Faith according to Paul is not an action of man, but a reaction following upon a divine action, and justification " out of " faith or " through " faith is in fact justification " in " faith, justification " in Christ," [3] justification " in the name of the Lord Jesus Christ," [4] justification " in His blood." [5] The formula " in (the) faith "

[1] LXX. Gen. 15. 6 (quoted by Paul in the form ἐπίστευσεν δὲ ’Αβραὰμ τῷ θεῷ καὶ ἐλογίσθη αὐτῷ εἰς δικαιοσύνην).

[2] ἐλογίσθη.   [3] Gal. 2. 17.   [4] 1 Cor. 6. 11.   [5] Rom. 5. 9.

AND THE FAITH OF PAUL 211

(ἐν (τῇ) πίστει) is often used by Paul: Gal. 2. 20; 1 Cor. 16. 13; 2 Cor. 13. 5; Col. 2. 7; and still more frequently in the Pastoral Epistles. It does not occur in combination with "justify" anywhere in the letters, as far as I can see, but that is an accident. The contrasted formula "in the law" (ἐν νόμῳ) is so combined in Gal. 3. 11; 5. 4. Faith is not the condition precedent to justification, it is the experience *of* justification.

Being justified in Christ, the believer possesses a "righteousness of God" in Christ.[1] This frequent technical expression[2] once replaced by the phrase "righteousness from God,"[3] is used by Paul to describe the normal condition of grace vouchsafed to us by God in Christ. That it is nothing of the nature of a magical transformation is shown by a passage in Galatians[4] which speaks of "waiting for" the desired righteousness. Before all men lies the last judgment, which

[1] 2 Cor. 5. 21, δικαιοσύνη Θεοῦ ἐν αὐτῷ.
[2] See also Rom. 1. 17 (not 3. 5); 3. 21, 22, 25, 26; 10. 3.
[3] Phil. 3. 9, τὴν ἐκ Θεοῦ δικαιοσύνην.
[4] Gal. 5. 5, ἡμεῖς γὰρ πνεύματι ἐκ πίστεως ἐλπίδα δικαιοσύνης ἀπεκδεχόμεθα.

will at length bring definitive justification. The justified man is therefore not a completely righteous man : he has still a goal of righteousness before him. In the Apostle's thoughts on justification as elsewhere we see the peculiar dynamic tension between the consciousness of present possession and the expectation of future full possession.

*

As an *enemy* [1] man stands before God in the second group of metaphors which clusters round the idea of " reconciliation " ; and in the marriage problem as treated by Paul, which contemplates the separation and reconciliation of a husband and wife,[2] we have a human example to help us to understand the figure. As an enemy man is alienated from God and far off from God ; [3] through Christ we became reconciled again with God.[4] We must not suppose that God is conciliated :

[1] Rom. 5. 10 ; Col. 1. 21, ἐχθροί; cf. Rom. 8. 7, ἔχθρα εἰς Θεόν.

[2] 1 Cor. 7. 11.

[3] Col. 1. 21, ἀπηλλοτριωμένους ; Eph. 2. 13, οἵ ποτε ὄντες μακρὰν.

[4] 2 Cor. 5. 18 ff. ; Rom. 5. 10.

AND THE FAITH OF PAUL 213

it is God [1] who changes us in Christ from enemies to persons reconciled. Therefore we have " peace with God through our Lord Jesus Christ " [2] or " the peace of God in Christ," [3] or, to sum up everything, " Christ is our peace." [4] It is perfectly clear that the " conception," often so highly dogmatised, of reconciliation in Paul coincides completely in meaning with the undogmatic idea of " peace." [5]

* * *

As a *debtor* man stands before God in the third cycle of metaphors,[6] in which the apostle is clearly following up the old Gospel estimate of sin as a debt.[7] In Christ the debtor experiences the remission of his debt,[8] for of His grace God presents us in Christ with the

[1] 2 Cor. 5. 18 ff. ; Col. 1. 20.
[2] Rom. 5. 1.
[3] Phil. 4. 7 ; cf. John 16. 33, " that in Me ye might have peace."
[4] Eph. 2. 14, αὐτὸς γάρ ἐστιν ἡ εἰρήνη ἡμῶν.
[5] Cf. especially Rom. 5. 1, compared with 5. 11.
[6] Cf. Col. 2. 14, τὸ καθ' ἡμῶν χειρόγραφον.
[7] Matt. 6. 12 ; Luke 11. 4.
[8] Col. 1. 14, ἄφεσιν τῶν ἁμαρτιῶν ; Eph. 1. 7, ἄφεσιν τῶν παραπτωμάτων.

amount of the debt which has grown up through our trespasses.[1] "Remission," that is the meaning of the word "forgiveness," and I do not believe that there is any great difference between the two Greek words which Paul uses.[2] Anyone who has seen one of the many acknowledgments of debt that have come down to us on papyrus from ancient times will realise that the metaphor which Paul carries out so remarkably of the bond nailed to the Cross, after being first blotted out and so cancelled,[3] was especially popular in its appeal.

* * *

And now comes the important series of metaphors, obviously valued and loved above others by the Apostle, which centres in the word "redemption." It is probably the most often misunderstood; but, viewed in connection with the civilisation of the ancient world in which Paul lived, there is no mis-

---

[1] Col. 2. 13, χαρισάμενος ἡμῖν πάντα τὰ παραπτώματα.
[2] ἄφεσις, Col. 1. 14; Eph. 1. 7; and πάρεσις, Rom. 3. 25.
[3] Col. 2. 14.

taking its simplicity and force. Though not immediately intelligible to us, this cycle of metaphors offered no difficulty at all to the ancient Christians, because it is connected with slavery, a social institution common to the whole of antiquity. It sees man standing as a *slave* before God, and there are various powers which Paul regards as the " masters " of the unfree man—sin,[1] the Law,[2] idols,[3] men,[4] death (corruption).[5] In Christ the slave obtains freedom.[6] This liberation of the slave in Christ [7] is suggested also by the word " redemption " : [8] as justification is the acquittal of the accused, so redemption is the emancipation of the slave by purchase. It is not improbable that Paul was following up a saying of Jesus to which he no doubt also alludes elsewhere : [9]

[1] Rom. 6. 6, 17, 19, 20 ; Tit. 3. 3.
[2] Gal. 4. 1–7 ; 5. 1.   [3] Gal. 4. 8, 9.
[4] 1 Cor. 7. 23.   [5] Rom. 8. 20 f.
[6] Gal. 2. 4. Cf. Gal. 5. 1 ; John 8. 36.
[7] Rom. 3. 24 ; Col. 1. 14 ; Eph. 1. 7.
[8] ἀπολύτρῶσις, 1 Cor. 1. 30 ; Rom. 3. 24 ; 8. 23 ; Col. 1. 14 ; Eph. 1. 7, 14 ; 4. 30.
[9] Phil. 2. 7, μορφὴν δούλου λαβών, " taking the form of a slave."

216   THE RELIGION OF JESUS

"The Son of man came not to be ministered unto, but to minister [as a slave], and to give His life a ransom for many [slaves]."[1]

The greatest impetus to the elaboration of metaphors of emancipation by purchase came, however, from the custom of sacral manumission, which was widely spread in the ancient world—and continued to be of effect among Hellenistic Jews and afterwards even among Christians—and with which we have once more become acquainted thanks chiefly to inscriptions.[2] Among the various legal forms by which, in the time of Paul, the manumission of a slave could take place we find the solemn rite of purchase of the slave by a deity. The owner comes with the slave to the temple, sells him there to the god, and receives from the temple treasury the purchase money, which the slave has previously deposited there out of his savings. The slave thus becomes the property of the god, but as against all the world he is a free man.

[1] Mark 10. 45 = Matt. 20. 28.
[2] See detailed evidence in *Light from the Ancient East*, pp. 323-334.

AND THE FAITH OF PAUL

From this point of view the words which twice occur in 1 Corinthians, "ye were bought with a price,"[1] like the sentence in Galatians about Christ redeeming them that were under the Law,[2] become vividly intelligible, especially when we see that Paul uses formulæ that recur regularly in inscriptions relating to manumissions, and when we remember that among the people to whom he wrote there were slaves who of course must have known all about that particular form of law. Having been freed through Christ or " in " Christ,[3] as " in " the temple of the god, those who have hitherto been the slaves of Sin, slaves of the Law, etc., are now slaves of Christ,[4] the property of Christ,[5] bondmen, incorporate with Christ,[6] but otherwise free men,[7] who must not be made slaves again.[8]

[1] 1 Cor. 6. 20 ; 7. 23, τιμῆς ἠγοράσθητε.
[2] Gal. 4. 5, ἵνα τοὺς ὑπὸ νόμου ἐξαγοράσῃ. Cf. 3. 13.
[3] Gal. 2. 4.
[4] Gal. 1. 10 ; Eph. 6. 6, and other passages.
[5] Gal. 3. 29 ; 5. 24 ; 1 Cor. 1. 12 [where I think you must put a stop after " Cephas," taking the next words to be Paul's rejoinder, " But I am Christ's "] ; 3. 23 ; 15. 23 ; 2 Cor. 10. 7.   [6] 1 Cor. 12. 27, etc.
[7] Gal. 5. 1, 13.   [8] Gal. 2. 4 ; 5. 1 ; 1 Cor. 7. 23.

The same contrast between the present possession and the future full possession which we found in the Apostle's assurance of justification can be also observed in his idea of redemption: those who have already been redeemed are still "waiting for" "the redemption of the body"; [1] "the day of redemption" is still before them. [2]

How little Paul binds himself dogmatically with this metaphor is shown by the fact that elsewhere he employs the figure of a *slave* for the sake of a different contrast: instead of slaves we become in Christ "sons of God." [3] Here Paul is employing the ancient legal conception of adoption. The Greek word he used [4] is not, as some scholars suggested, an invention of Paul, but a technical term of ancient Greek law, very often found in inscriptions.

The adoption by God which we have experienced in Christ is, after all, still the

[1] Rom. 8. 23, υἱοθεσίαν ἀπεκδεχόμενοι, τὴν ἀπολύτρωσιν τοῦ σώματος.

[2] Eph. 4. 30, ἐν ᾧ ἐσφραγίσθητε εἰς ἡμέραν, ἀπολυτρώσεως.

[3] υἱοὶ Θεοῦ, Gal. 4. 5 f.; 3. 26; Rom. 8. 14.

[4] υἱοθεσία.

object of our expectation, we still wait for the adoption.[1]

We shall not comprehend Paul until we have heard all these various testimonies concerning Salvation in Christ sounding together in harmony like the notes of a single full choral. To ask "what is the relation of justification to reconciliation in Paulinism?" is absolutely useless. Such a question has no more value than to ask: "what is the relation of an accused person to an enemy?" We have understood those great confessions of the great Christian when we have read them, no, not read, but heard them like the immortal sounds of a fugue of Bach.

Reviewing these Pauline pictures of salvation in communion with Christ, I should like to make two observations. The first is concerned with the sociological peculiarity of this Pauline use of similes; the other concerns their practical value in preaching and instruction.

[1] Rom. 8. 23, υἱοθεσίαν ἀπεκδεχόμενοι ("waiting for the adoption").

All the Pauline similes show that he had a good understanding of the ancient ideas of Law. They indicate to us also that he was used to the atmosphere of great cities. In this there lies a great difference between his use of similes and that of Jesus. Jesus drew His illustrations more from the life in the fields, villages, and small towns. Taking him altogether, Paul belongs to the great city. You know the saying about the great founders of the orders of monks:—

"Bernhardus valles, Benedictus montes amabat,
Oppida Franciscus, celebres Ignatius urbes."

"Bernard loved the valleys, Benedict the mountains, Francis loved the small towns, Ignatius loved the famous cities."

The differences between Paul and Ignatius are certainly great, but Paul, like Ignatius, belongs to the great city, and one may say that the great architect who built St. Paul's in London, with the divining power of the artist, discovered the right situation for a church of St. Paul.

The illustrations of Paul are, if one may use the expression with regard to him, thoroughly modern. To illustrate the great subject of salvation in Christ, Paul used pictures, which were understandable to every one of the simplest people of his own day, and some of which are even to-day without further explanation understandable. In this lies an indication of the method of our modern evangelisation; the technique of our language of illustration must fit our own time. I have the impression that among the English-speaking peoples there are preachers who have a great gift for using such modern similes. The Pauline illustrations will be more satisfactorily adapted to our own times the less we petrify them into dogmatic statements, and the more we see them as expressions of living religion.

IV

THE NEW CREATION IN COMMUNION WITH CHRIST. THE FELLOWSHIP OF THE SUFFERINGS OF CHRIST

In the third lecture we spoke of salvation in communion with Christ. When we speak to-day of the new creation in communion with Christ, this is not strictly speaking a new chapter—certainly not a new chapter in Pauline dogmatic. Rather it is a new chord in the Pauline oratorio. Paul did not work out a complicated dogmatic system shewing how the grace of God in Christ had brought about and continued to bring salvation to men, but in a fulness of similes, he expressed the one great experience of salvation.

The impression of complexity has only arisen because we have not understood the similes as similes which were synonymous with one another, though to the mind of antiquity they would easily have been so understood. The single so-called Pauline ideas have been isolated by us, and then the attempt has

THE FAITH OF PAUL

been made to reconstruct a chronological order of salvation, an "*ordo salutis*," as our ancestors called it. As a matter of fact, the religion of Paul is something quite simple. It is communion with Christ. In Christ, the unfathomable mysteries of God's mercy become clear to him: that is his experience of salvation. In Christ, he comes to an entirely different judgment of himself, and that is the New Creation.

Paul answered two questions for himself: What has God done? and, What have I experienced? In the earlier lecture we gave an answer to the first question, and have touched upon the more objective side of the divine revelation of salvation. To-day, we intend to answer the second question, touching thereby on the more subjective side of the matter.

"*New Creation.*" Paul was specially gifted in the coining of clear-cut phrases. It is a great misunderstanding of Paul to suppose that the long periods, which occur, for instance, in the Epistle to the Romans, are characteristic of his style. I believe when

Paul composed these long periods it was because the development of his thought was halting. In his great creative moments he succeeded in expressing himself in monumental lines of extraordinary conciseness and power. Once in a Berlin Greek Society, I read Heraclitus with some friends of mine and was reminded by his style, on several points, of Paul. It would not be difficult from the Pauline epistles to gather together a collection of such monumental sayings ; for example, " The letter killeth, but the spirit gives life ; " [1] " The Jews ask for signs, the Greeks seek after wisdom ; " [2] " The kingdom of God is not in word, but in power ; " [3] " Knowledge puffeth up, but love edifieth ; " [4] " The Spirit searcheth all things, yea, the deep things of

[1] 2 Cor. 3. 6, τὸ γὰρ γράμμα ἀποκτέννει, τὸ δὲ πνεῦμα ζωοποιεῖ. This saying is fittingly placed over the door of the University Library in Heidelberg ; it is only a pity that they have there replaced the vulgar form ἀποκτέννει by the classic form ἀποκτείνει.

[2] 1 Cor. 1. 22, Ἰουδαῖοι σημεῖα αἰτοῦσιν καὶ Ἕλληνες σοφίαν ζητοῦσιν.

[3] 1 Cor. 4. 20, οὐ γὰρ ἐν λόγῳ ἡ βασιλεία τοῦ Θεοῦ ἀλλ' ἐν δυνάμει.

[4] 1 Cor. 8, 1, ἡ γνῶσις φυσιοῖ, ἡ δὲ ἀγάπη οἰκοδομεῖ.

God." [1] If it had happened that Paul had only been known to us through a collection of a few such fragments, then, simply on account of such phrases, we should have to reckon him among the greatest minds of antiquity.

To this class of great, important sayings, full of meaning, belongs the passage, "Therefore if any man be in Christ, he is a new creation;" or: "therefore if any man be in Christ, he is a new creature." [2]

I think there lies in this confession a clear reflection of Paul's conversion experience. As I have before expressed it, we may read here the second page of the Pauline Genesis, on the first page of which was written the sudden blaze of light near Damascus.

Living in Christ, Paul divides his life into two great periods, that of the old Paul, and that of the Paul newly created.[3] The "old man"[4] had lived in other spheres. Allow

[1] 1 Cor. 2. 10, τὸ γὰρ πνεῦμα πάντα ἐραυνᾷ, καὶ τὰ βάθη τοῦ Θεοῦ.
[2] 2 Cor. 5. 17, εἴ τις ἐν Χριστῷ καινὴ κτίσις.
[3] 2 Cor. 5. 17.
[4] Rom. 6. 6; Eph. 4. 22, ὁ παλαιὸς (ἡμῶν ἄνθρωπος).

me to remind you of the hints given in the first lecture concerning those parallel and contrasted formulæ, coined in similar form to the formulæ " in Christ " : " in the Flesh " ;[1] " in Sins " ;[2] " in Adam,"[3] with his death-appointed destiny ; " in the Law " ;[4] " in the World " ;[5] " in Sufferings."[6] The " new man "[7] in Christ stands within the sacred precinct, into which all those gloomy things of the past cannot penetrate :—

> " The old things are passed away ;
> Behold they are become new."[8]

Let us now consider the single experiences of the new man Paul.

The flesh has no power over the new man, because as a follower of Christ he has " crucified " the flesh.[9]

We shall have more to say of this peculiar Pauline thought presently.

As a new creature Paul the Christian is

---

[1] Rom. 7. 5 ; 8. 8, 9.   [2] 1 Cor. 15. 17.
[3] 1 Cor. 15. 22.
[4] Gal. 5. 4 ; Rom. 3. 19 ; 2. 12, ἐν τῷ νόμῳ.
[5] Eph. 2. 12.   [6] 2 Cor. 6. 4.
[7] Col. 3. 10, τὸν νέον ἄνθρωπον.
[8] 2 Cor. 5. 17.   [9] Gal. 5. 24.

also free from sin.[1] He has been loosed from sin—*but*, is he also sinless, incapable of sinning? In theory certainly Paul might subscribe to the statement that the Christian does not sin.[2] But the awful experiences of practice would give him cause to doubt. Paul the shepherd of souls retained a sober judgment; freedom from sin is not conceived of as something mechanical and magical. Side by side with all his moral exhortations to Christians to battle against sin there are confessions of Paul the Christian himself, especially in his letter to the Romans,[3] witnessing that even the new-created feels at times the old deep sense of sin. But in Christ the grace of God is daily vouchsafed to him anew, and daily he experiences anew the renovating creative power of that grace.

The new Paul is also rid of that fellowship with Adam which is a fellowship of death.[4] He is no longer " in Adam," but " in Christ,"

[1] Rom. 6. 1–14.
[2] See Rom. 6. 2, 6, 11. Compare the corresponding Johannine confessions, 1 John 3. 6, 9; 5. 18.
[3] Particularly Rom. 7.
[4] 1 Cor. 15. 22; Rom. 5. 12 ff.

and in Christ he has the guarantee that death has been overcome.[1]

Paul the Christian is also a new creature because in Christ he is free from the Law: "Christ is the end of the Law."[2]

The "letter" is overcome by the "spirit."[3] The problem of the Law was especially torturing to the former Pharisee, and it occupies a large amount of space in the letters owing to Paul's polemical position with regard to the Judaisers. But it was not solved by one single statement in round terms. It is a true paradox that Paul the antinomist remained a pious Bible Christian and could still upon occasion quote the words of the Law as an authority. His polemic against the Law, though often harsh,[4] seeks to preserve for the Law at least a portion of its dignity.[5] Freedom from the slavery of the Law is conceived in no sense favourable to libertinism.[6]

---

[1] I Cor. 15. 22.   [2] Rom. 10. 4.

[3] Rom. 7. 6; 2 Cor. 3. 6.

[4] The worst is probably the polemic against Moses in 2 Cor. 3. 13 f.

[5] Cf. especially Gal. 3. 21 ff.

[6] Gal. 5. 13.

Like Jesus,[1] Paul proclaims that the quintessence of the Law is contained in the commandment to love one's neighbour.[2]

This freedom from the Law stands in Paul's Epistles strongly in the foreground. It has an outer basis, and an inner one. It was necessary for Paul to speak a great deal about the Law, in view of the anti-Judaic polemic that was forced upon him, as I have mentioned before. But for him personally, too, the Law had been an inner matter of extraordinary importance from his earliest childhood. Even in his old age there stood out clearly to his soul one experience of his childhood, concerning which he gives pathetic hints in his letter to the Romans. We might speak of it as his fall :—

" For I was alive without the law once : but when the commandment came, sin revived, and I died. And the commandment, which was ordained to life, I found to be unto death. For sin, taking occasion by the commandment, deceived me, and by it slew me." [3]

[1] Matt. 22. 39 and parallels.
[2] Gal. 5. 14 ; Rom. 13. 8.   [3] Rom. 7. 9–11.

Paul is probably thinking here in the first place of his earliest childhood, which he elsewhere [1] describes as the time of childish immaturity; the idea of " sin " and the sense of guilt were both still unknown to him. But then came a sad day that he could never forget. In the Synagogue the child had seen from afar with awe and curiosity the solemn rolls of the Law in their brilliant embroidered coverings,[2] but now for the first time the " thou shalt " of the Law, conveyed to him, no doubt, by the mouth of a parent, entered commandingly into his consciousness. The Law's " thou shalt " was, however, closely followed by the child's " I will not " and transgression. Paul does not say what the occasion was. But he indicates that this first sin wrought terrible havoc in his sensitive young soul: he felt himself deceived; it was as if he had tasted death :—" I died."

We do not know when this tragedy took place in the soul of the youthful Paul; many of us know from personal experience what agony the sense of guilt can cause even in

[1] 1 Cor. 13. 11.   [2] 2 Cor. 3. 14.

childish years. Jewish teachers, at least of a later period, seem to have assumed [1] that a child grew to the age of nine without knowing anything of sin; but that then, with the awakening of the " evil instinct," sin began. More important, however, than the explanation of this experience in detail is the fact which, I think can be certainly concluded from it. The man who experienced this fall cannot have had a sunny, happy youth; the Law, sin, and death had already cast their gloomy shadows upon the soul of the gifted boy, and the prevailing tone of his mind as he gradually matured into the conscious Jew may be described, according to his own indication, as one of slavish anxiety [2]—that is, not merely the fear of God in the old Biblical sense,[3] but the deep distress of one "born under the Law [4] concerning his soul's salvation:—

" O wretched man that I am! Who shall deliver me out of this body of death?" [5]

[1] Tanchuma (late commentary on the Pentateuch) on Gen. 3. 22.
[2] Rom. 8. 15.   [3] 2 Cor. 7. 1; Rom. 3. 18.   [4] Gal. 4. 4.
[5] Rom. 7. 24, ταλαίπωρος ἐγὼ ἄνθρωπος· τίς με ῥύσεται ἐκ τοῦ σώματος τοῦ θανάτου τούτου;

Even in his Christian period Paul is capable of such cries for help when the old distress wakes in him again.

I do not regard it as right to separate these appalling phrases from Paul himself, as if he were not speaking of his own inner life, but were only explaining in a quiet way some theological example of dogmatic facts of general application. Rather these sentences are real confessions, and justify us in suggesting that Paul, living " in Law," had very nearly approached the acting type of mystic, while the Paul living " in Christ " was an example of the reacting mystic.[1]

[1] I had just written down this sentence when I received a question by this morning's post, which what I have just said answers. The questioner also asks with regard to the more general problem of mysticism, whether I agree that the acting mystic is interested in his own feelings, while the reacting mystic seeks communion with God through the more complete experience of understanding, emotion and service. In general, I agree with this differentiation. I would perhaps formulate it somewhat differently.

The acting mystic is interested in the increase of his spiritual experiences, through special methods.

The reacting mystic seeks communion with God through more complete experience of understanding

How high the new Paul felt himself to be elevated above the " world " and its Satanic and dæmonic powers, is shown by many powerful sayings whose force depends on the sense they convey of personal union with Christ. The mightiest song of triumph is surely that in his letter to the Romans.[1]

He who does not understand the bearing of this " in Christ " in Paul's religion, should let this psalm (which is really a piece of the Pauline oratorio) sink into his mind.

* * *

If we turn now to Paul's expression of " the fellowship of the sufferings of Christ." we thereby touch upon a singularity of Pauline religion that is as important and as peculiar as it is comparatively little noticed. In every

---

and service, and regards the emotion that he experiences in connection with this as the gift of God's grace, but it is not the emotion that he especially seeks. When he says : " I have understanding of God," that really means : " I have been understood by God." Cf. I Cor. 13. 12 : " Then shall I know, even as also I have been known ; " compare also Gal. 4. 9 : " Now after that ye have known God, or rather are known of God, how turn ye again to the weak and beggarly elements ? "

[1] Rom. 8. 35-39.

religion we find some sort of an attitude taken up to the problem of suffering, and several great answers to this problem run through a number of religions, and are found also in Christianity. Suffering is traced back to a power opposed to God. We find this solution, which has come about through an act of intellectual resignation, even in Christianity. Or suffering is regarded as punishment sent by God for the sin of men; or suffering is in the hand of God the means of trying and purifying men. All these attitudes towards suffering are also found in Paul. But it is particularly noteworthy that he also discovered an entirely new attitude to suffering.

In all the before-mentioned answers to the problem of suffering, suffering is regarded as something abnormal, and the answers have this in common, that they come to terms with the fact which cannot be denied. They have the character of a compromise. The peculiarity of the Pauline attitude is this, that he has dared the paradox of regarding suffering in communion with Christ as something quite normal and necessary.

AND THE FAITH OF PAUL 235

Paul has the conviction that "in Christ" he is in an especial way elevated above suffering. In this connection he gave form to one of the deepest, most pregnant conceptions that we owe to him: for since he suffers in Christ, his sufferings are to him "sufferings of Christ"[1] or "afflictions of Christ."[2]

It is exceedingly important that we rightly understand these Pauline technical expressions "the sufferings of Christ" and "the afflictions of Christ." I would remind you that we saw in the first lecture that the genitive "of Christ" is not a subjective genitive, but a mystic genitive. In one passage of Paul's letters, dogmatic exegesis has made a very great mistake: "Now I rejoice in my sufferings for your sake, and fill up on my part that which is lacking of the afflictions of Christ in my flesh for his body's sake, which is the Church."[3] This has been explained thus: Paul took it that the historical Christ had to

[1] "Christ-sufferings," 2 Cor. 1. 5; Phil. 3. 10.
[2] "Christ-afflictions," Col. 1. 24.
[3] Col. 1. 24: νῦν χαίρω ἐν τοῖς παθήμασιν ὑπὲρ ὑμῶν, καὶ ἀνταναπληρῶ τὰ ὑστερήματα τῶν θλίψεων τοῦ Χριστοῦ ἐν τῇ σαρκί μου ὑπὲρ τοῦ σώματος αὐτοῦ, ὅ ἐστιν ἡ ἐκκλησία.

bear a certain definite amount of suffering according to the will of God, but that He had not borne all this suffering in His historical Passion. A remainder was still left to be borne. It was therefore the task of Paul to bear this remainder which Christ had not borne.

That is a quite mistaken explanation. The true sense is rather this: I, Paul, have, as a member of the body of Christ, a certain amount of suffering to bear according to the will of God. Already I have borne much of this, and a remainder of my "afflictions of Christ" is still left for me to bear. So the term "afflictions of Christ" means the same as the term "my sufferings." The peculiarity and delicateness of this thought is that the sufferings of Paul are "sufferings of Christ." This conviction can be made even clearer if we alter the Pauline saying: "I live, yet not I, but Christ liveth in me"[1] into "I suffer, yet not I, but Christ suffers in me."

This whole complex of thought about the fellowship of the sufferings of Christ is to be

[1] Gal. 3. 20.

understood from the standpoint of the Pauline Christology. At the commanding centre of Paul's contemplation of Christ there stands the Living One who is also the Crucified, or the Crucified who is also alive. The death on the cross and the resurrection of Christ cannot in Paul be isolated as two distinct facts; as contemplated by him they are inseparably connected. This is shown even linguistically; the Greek perfect participle for "crucified" might be rendered "He who is the Crucified."[1]

This language of the cult is found already in the Gospels.[2] This Greek perfect participle goes a great way farther than the aorist, which would be equivalent to "He who was crucified,"[3] and which Paul never applied to Christ in his letters.[4] The perfect tense, no

[1] ἐσταυρωμένος, Gal. 3. 1; 1 Cor. 1. 23; 2. 2.
[2] Mark 16. 6; cf. Matt. 28. 5.   [3] σταυρωθείς.
[4] Once only he employs the aorist indicative, ἐσταυρώθη (2 Cor. 13. 4), but here he is not speaking of the present beneficent efficacy of the crucifixion: Christ, he says, was crucified (at that time in the past) through weakness. The crass materialism of after-generations is shown in the watchword of a later controversy, "God who was crucified" (Θεὸς ὁ σταυρωθείς).

doubt, indicates that the cross is not a bare fact in the historic past, but something whose influence is continued into the present ; " the Crucified " is a reality which can be experienced every day, and the Johannine picture [1] of the Living One who bears the wounds of the Crucified is as much Pauline as the double meaning of the Johannine word " lift up," [2] which indicates at one and the same time the death on the lofty cross and the " exaltation " to spiritual glory in the sense of the passage in Philippians.[3]

I would make another observation akin to this. Paul's use of the phrase " the blood of Christ," as a term characteristic of the cult, corresponds to his conviction of the identity of the Living One with the Crucified.[4] The term " blood of Christ," in many passages at least, does not refer to the physical blood once shed at the historic martyrdom ; it is a

[1] John 20. 27. [2] John 12. 32, 33 ; 3. 14 ; 8. 28.
[3] Phil. 2. 9.
[4] On what follows I refer to Otto Schmitz, *Die Opferanschauung des späteren Judentums und die Opferaussagen des Neuen Testamentes*, Tübingen, 1910, pp. 214 ff. Compare also above, p. 179.

vivid way of realising the Living One who is also the Crucified, and with whom we live in mystic spiritual " fellowship of Blood." [1]

Here, too, the Apostle expresses the conviction that he stands in a fellowship of suffering, a fellowship of the cross, and a fellowship of life with the spiritual Christ. In many passages the formula " in the blood of Christ " borders upon the formula " in Christ " and might be translated appropriately to the sense, " in the fellowship of blood with Christ." [2]

Reviewing all this we see that the suffering Paul is not the old Paul but the new Paul, who is a member of the Body of Christ, and who therefore shares mystically in all that that Body experienced and now experiences: he " suffers with Christ," [3] is " crucified with Christ,"[4] " dies,"[5] is " buried,"[6] is " raised,"[7] and " lives "[8] with Christ. Thus suffering is

[1] 1 Cor. 10. 16.
[2] Rom. 3. 25; cf. Eph. 1. 7; Rom. 5. 9; cf. 5. 10; Eph. 2. 13.
[3] Rom. 8. 17.   [4] Gal. 2. 20.
[5] Rom. 6. 8; cf. Col. 2. 20; 3. 3; 2 Tim. 2. 11.
[6] Rom. 6. 4; cf. Col. 2. 12.
[7] Col. 2. 12; cf. 3. 3; Rom. 6. 4 f.
[8] Rom. 6. 8; cf. 2 Tim. 2. 11.

not an anomaly in Paul's life, but, being the suffering of Christ, it is a normal part of his state as a Christian, and a certain fixed measure of " afflictions of Christ " must, as we saw, according to God's plan be " filled up " by him.[1]

In this Pauline mysticism of suffering it is easy to recognise what I have called the undogmatic element in Paul. Dogmatic exegesis is puzzled by such passages; it tortures itself to find a meaning in them, and yet cannot express the inwardness of the mystic contemplation of suffering in theological formulæ. But under the cross of Jesus a suffering man will be able even to-day to experience for himself the depth of meaning and the comfort implied by Paul's " sufferings of Christ." Similarly the ancient Christians were easily able to comprehend the mystic application of the several stages of baptism [2] to death, burial, and resurrection with Christ, because, having been baptised as adults, they had an indelibly vivid recollection of the

[1] Col. 1. 24.
[2] Rom. 6. 3 ff.; Col. 2. 12.

AND THE FAITH OF PAUL

ceremony as performed on them by immersion.

* * *

It is an extraordinarily interesting task in the history of religion, to investigate the possible analogies to this in other religions. Among the religions of antiquity, there are especially the Osiris-cult, the Adonis-cult, and the Attis-cult to be investigated. A task of equal importance is to investigate the parallel ideas that have developed in Christianity, and some which have possibly come without any Pauline influence. The literature concerning the Passion, especially the preaching of the Passion, and the treatment of the Passion in art, in painting and sculpture as well as in music, offer us rich material ready to hand for the history of the Christian Passion mysticism.

Everywhere Passion mysticism is to be recognised in the fact that the sufferings of Christ are not regarded as something in the past only, but also as something which is still going on; and that is the meaning of the innumerable artistic representations of the Passion. They attempt to realise in the present the Passion of the Saviour. Without regard to this, neither the Oberammergau Passion Play nor the Passion music of Bach can be understood. The meaning of these great creations is not simply to picture a historical fact of the past, but rather to bring the souls of the audience to regard the Passion of Jesus as something that is still present, working upon us and transforming us. Christ-cult and Christ-mysticism here are very close together. What one may call the dogmatical treatment of the Passion is separated from these by a great gulf.

Many of us have experienced the enormous difficulty which lay in many lines of the hymns about the Passion that we had to learn as children. These difficulties came in part certainly from this fact, that we have interpreted by the dogmatic method poetry that was meant mystically. Paul himself, as I suggested before, has been sacrificed to this false interpretation. The beginning of the sixth chapter of Romans for example is, when interpreted in this dogmatic way, an unescapable stumbling-block. I do not know if any composer of an oratorio has used these lines of Romans in his work. It appears to me that if they were sung, they would at once lose much of their difficulty.

Perhaps I may quite shortly mention one example of a true understanding of the Pauline Passion mysticism. In the room of my New Testament Seminar at Berlin there hangs a picture—a great painting of Garofalo, an Italian artist of the time of the Renaissance. The Crucified is there; by His cross, the world and the history of the world is divided into two great parts. On the left of the Crucified is the Synagogue, in the shape of a sorrowing woman, the fallen Temple of Solomon, and the High Priest with his cult already coming to an end. Under the right arm of the Crucified is the Church, in the shape of a queenly woman, surrounded by the four Evangelists, and by the side is the Areopagus and Paul preaching there. The remarkable feature of the picture is this : from the wound in the side of the Crucified there comes a stream of blood. It goes like a red band through the hand of the Church, and underneath is divided into three streams, each of which streams constitutes a Sacrament. Here it is obvious that the ruling idea is the mystical one. The Crucified is thought of as living, and His blood as a divine, living reality.

I can fully understand it, if anyone feels that this whole mystical world is strange to him. But if one wishes to understand the great creations of the past, one must see them above all things in their own spiritual surroundings. The spiritual environment of the Pauline Passion mysticism, and of Paul's mysticism in general, is not the modern Western scholar's study, but the open air and light of the Holy East, and its source is not the intellect concerned in formulating a thesis, and propounding midnight hypotheses at its study table, but a prophetic mind trembling in the presence of God.

V

CHRIST-MYSTICISM AND ETHICS. LATER DEVELOPMENTS FROM THE PAULINE COMMUNION WITH CHRIST

THE longer and oftener that we have spoken of the Christ-mysticism of Paul, the more pressing becomes a certain problem, upon the answering of which in the end our whole attitude to Paul is dependent. What is the relationship of Mysticism to Ethics in Paul?

One who knew mysticism only from its caricatures, having no inner experience of it, might very likely, with oppression of heart, put the question like this: " After all, is not this communion with Christ only the bewildered dream of an over-heated Oriental phantasy, or the fixed idea of a pathological brain ? Is it not the drunkenness of an ecstatic, who seeks only his own enjoyment, a drunkenness from which a gaping idler wakes, who is useless for the great problems of the day ? "

Our characterisation of the Pauline mysticism as a reacting mysticism seems to bring these suggestions into the region of probability. A reacting mystic might be one who simply allowed himself to be the will-less instrument of some indefinable higher power. Reacting mysticism appears to exclude the true spontaneous activity of the self. I believe that many conceive Paul as a mystic from this side, as a soft, weak, fantastic dreamer, as a crazy visionary who is useless for the world because the power of his will has been doped with narcotics.

This picture is certainly mistaken. Quite apart from any personal confessions in his letters, a glance at the work of his life is enough to give the verdict: Paul was a man of a quite extraordinary activity. The merely physical work of travel which Paul performed was enormous; and when we realise that he suffered from a severe chronic ailment, and was therefore weakened by that as well as by ill-treatment and privation, we may well be astounded at his achievement.

But from his letters we can give full proof

AND THE FAITH OF PAUL 247

that Paul himself was quite aware of the danger of mystical excitement alone, and that his reacting mysticism was, as a matter of fact, united with an active ethic of unparalleled intensity.

Before we enter further upon these two points, I might also add that the history of mysticism indicates that acting mystics have as ethical subjects often been most inactive, and that reacting mystics, as ethical subjects, have often been uncommonly active. Paul was a reacting mystic to such an extent that, in that religious activity, which of all seems to be most natural to the religious mind, in prayer, he felt himself in the end to be carried along by God. We gather that Paul, at the highest point of his prayer life, experienced that he did not pray himself, but that God gave him the prayer.[1] But even this experience did not injure his ethical standpoint.

That Paul himself recognised the dangers of the purely mystical excitement, he himself indicates in several places. The problem

[1] Rom. 8. 26.

of the relation between Mysticism and Ethics stood clearly before his soul, though he never formulated it in such a doctrinaire fashion. Here, especially, the First Epistle to the Corinthians is the classical document. I will only mention some of the most important testimonies, from which it is clear that the contrast between mysticism and ethics was well known to him. He speaks of mystical prayer and speaking with tongues, and declares that the personal experience of mystical enjoyment is valueless in comparison with the ethical edification of the congregation.

" For thou verily givest thanks well, but the other is not edified. I thank God I speak with tongues more than you all; howbeit, in the church, I had rather speak five words with my understanding, that I might instruct others also, than ten thousand words in a tongue." [1]

Also in the saying, " Knowledge puffeth up, but love edifieth," [2] we have the contrast between mystical knowledge and active love. Similarly, also, " to know the love of Christ which passeth knowledge." [3] The classical

[1] 1 Cor. 14. 17, 18. [2] 1 Cor. 8. 1. [3] Eph. 3. 19.

monument of this ethical soberness of Paul the Mystic, is 1 Corinthians 13, the hymn of love. In this hymn, a mystic and ecstatic places mysticism and ecstasy definitely on a lower level than ethics. All the gifts of the Spirit—speaking with tongues, prophecy, knowledge, faith, charity and martyrdom—are of no value without love, and by " love " he means love to one's neighbour. With the already-mentioned gift of coining his ideas in short, clear phrases, he gave the answer to this problem. We might refer again to the words : " Wherefore if any man is in Christ, he is a new creature," [1] for we can use this term " new creature," not simply to indicate the new religious man, but also the new ethical man in Paul. Even clearer is the statement : " I can do all things in Him that strengtheneth me." [2] But most precisely of all is the whole question answered in the sentence : " In Christ . . . availeth faith, working through love." [3] What we, in our study call Mysticism, the great religious practical man called Faith ; and what we call Ethics, he called Love.

[1] 2 Cor. 5. 17.   [2] Phil. 4. 13.   [3] Gal. 5. 6.

For this ethical, fundamental idea, Love, he also fashioned a technical term, " love of Christ." What is " love of Christ " ? Once again we must think of our old friend " the mystical genitive." " Love of Christ " is the same as " love in Christ "—that is, love to the neighbour the effective power of which springs from communion with Christ. I believe that " to know the love of Christ that passeth knowledge," [1] is to be understood in this sense.

The risen Christ, the spirit of Christ in Paul, gives him power, not only in the experience of redemption, and so forth, but, because He Himself *is* Love, there streams over Paul from communion with Him, the power of love as the power of ethical action. This, with Paul, is " love of Christ." Paul's religious contemplation is not the only thing to be explained by the fellowship with Christ. The store of ethical convictions which he

[1] Eph. 3. 19; About the two other places, 2 Cor. 5. 14 and Rom. 8. 35,

" For the love of Christ constraineth us."

" Who shall separate us from the love of Christ ? " we may be in some doubt whether this meaning is to be accepted.

brought with him from Judaism and the Hellenistic world, and which was very greatly increased by Gospel traditions, acquires its real brilliance through the experience of communion with Christ. Even the ethical element in Paul is made fast to Christ; " the love of Christ " is the power for good which the individual possesses, and the power of goodness which permeates the whole organisation of Christendom.

* * *

This latter, the element of social ethics in Paul, is unmistakably religious in tone. He is most fond of regarding the community of believers under three aspects—as a family, as a body, and as a temple. Each of these metaphors is given a religious setting.

Christians are a family because God is their Father, and Christ as the " firstborn " Son of God is their Brother,[1] whose rights to the inheritance they share.[2] Differences of nation, rank, and sex are of no more account " in Christ " :—

[1] Rom. 8. 29. [2] Rom. 8. 17.

> "Therein is neither Jew nor Greek,
> Therein is neither slave nor freeman,
> Therein is no male and female :
> For ye are all one man in Christ Jesus." [1]

Of course the religious gulf between Jews and non-Jews is bridged over :—

> " Wherein there is no Greek and Jew,
> Circumcision and uncircumcision,
> Barbarian, Scythian, slave, freeman,
> But Christ is all and in all." [2]

But he raises himself to the high vision that in Christ the barriers of enmity between the peoples are broken down : " For He is our peace who hath made both one, and hath broken down the middle wall of partition between us." [3] So Paul may even be regarded as the creator of a world-wide ethic of humanity.

Regarding the community as the family of God, Paul took the name of " brother " very seriously : " The brother for whose sake Christ died," [4] " Him for whom Christ died." [5] With such irresistible words as these he stamps even the most insignificant comrade with a

---
[1] Gal. 3. 28. [2] Col. 3. 11. [3] Eph. 2. 14.
[4] 1 Cor. 8. 11. [5] Rom. 14. 15.

value for eternity, and impresses upon the indifference of the " strong " Christians [1] of Corinth and Rome the duty of tender brotherly consideration, making all Christians together collectively responsible for the mutual care of souls :—

" Brethren, even if a man be overtaken in any trespass, ye which are spiritual restore such a one in a spirit of meekness ; looking to thyself, lest thou also be tempted. Bear ye one another's burdens, and so fulfil the law of Christ." [2]

But of course the most striking memorial of Paul's sense of brotherhood is the " way " which he showed unto the Corinthians, the Song of Songs about brotherly love [3] :—

" If I speak with the tongues of men and of angels,
But have not love,
I am become sounding brass
Or a clanging cymbal."—

Christians are a " body," and the Head is Christ, or Christ is the Body, and Christians

[1] Rom. 15. 1.   [2] Gal. 6. 1, 2.
[3] 1 Cor. 12. 31 and 13.

are the members.[1] Paul has here Christianised a well-known metaphor of which the ancients were very fond. His idea of the body of Christ, combined with the idea of Christian solidarity, profound in its simplicity, was passed on by him to assist the progress of the future Church.

The figure is no less popular when both the individual Christian [2] and the Church [3] are spoken of as a " temple " which is still building, and which, though already inhabited by God, requires continual building up (edification). Paul had seen such unfinished temples on his journeys, in Jerusalem and in Asia Minor. The temple of Herod was not quite finished until the sixties of the first century, a short time before it was destroyed. In Asia Minor on the site of excavations among the ruins of ancient temples I have seen again and again unfinished materials of ancient date which had never received the last stroke of the mason's mallet. . . .

---

[1] Col. 1. 18, 24 ; 2. 19 ; Eph. 4. 15 f. ; 5. 23 ; 1 Cor. 12. 12 ; Rom. 12. 4 ff. [2] 1 Cor. 6. 19.
[3] 1 Cor. 3. 16 ff. ; 2 Cor. 6. 16 ; Eph. 2. 20 ff.

Like the medieval cathedrals, these Anatolian temples required " edification " by the work of generations : hence the explanation of Paul's favourite idea of " edification," which has acquired special importance in 1 and 2 Corinthians. We see the work going forward once more on the site where the new Christian community is being built up :—

" According to the grace of God which was given unto me, as a wise master builder I laid a foundation ; and another buildeth thereon. But let each man take heed how he buildeth thereon. For other foundation can no man lay than that which is laid, which is Jesus Christ. But if any man buildeth on the foundation gold, silver, costly stones, wood, hay, reed ; each man's work shall be made manifest : for the day shall declare it, because it is revealed in fire ; and the fire itself shall prove each man's work of what sort it is." [1]

There are incapable persons who, instead of a temple that defies the fire, built of fine stone, and decorated with gold and silver, can only manage to erect light wooden sheds or even miserable huts of straw or reed. Paul, the city-resident, who no doubt on his

[1] 1 Cor. 3. 10–13.

journeys had often seen wretched habitations of this kind reduced to ashes in a moment, did not want the Church of Christ to resemble them. The solid foundation, the like of which had never been seen, deserved to be crowned with a massive, noble edifice.

Nevertheless, Paul was far from formulating a fixed " conception of the Church " that would satisfy a lawyer. The Apostle cannot be called the father of the constitutional church. His churches were " assemblies " summoned by God—God's levy. All of them together are spoken of as " the assembly," [1] and the single assemblies sometimes possessed also " house-assemblies," [2] that is, smaller fellowships meeting for edification at certain houses. In all these brotherhoods, smaller or greater, breathes the Spirit, perceptible in the wondrous effects produced, and bestowing on every brother the special grace (charisma) that the assembly needs. The first letter to the Corinthians is classical

[1] ἐκκλησία, 1 Cor. 10. 32 ; 12. 28; Col. 1. 18, 24, etc.
[2] ἡ ἐκκλησία κατ' οἶκον, 1 Cor. 16. 19 ; Col. 4. 15; Philem. 2. ; Rom. 16. 5.

AND THE FAITH OF PAUL

evidence of this "charismatic" age before the days of the organised Church.

* * *

The moral personality of Paul is reflected in hundreds of ethical commands and words of advice. His letters are a witness how wide and how manly his ethical ideal was; they are full of detached moral exhortations. Problems of the day came before this great pastor in plenty, and he settled them all from the certainty of his fellowship with Christ, and always in the light of the Gospel. But no one should make of these scattered detached sayings a Pauline "system of ethics," and we must most certainly avoid the mistake of saying that things which happen not to be mentioned in the letters lay "beyond his ethical horizon." Here too we must repeat, the letters are fragments. Nor is Paul a professed ethical theorist; like other great spiritual guides, in important questions of ethical principle he felt no necessity to harmonise his principles with one another: everything comes from God, from Christ, through the Spirit, and yet Paul believes man is capable of everything. Determinists and indeterminists can therefore both appeal to his authority ; Paul himself was neither the one nor the other : to him the oar was as valuable as the sail :—

"So then, my beloved, even as ye have always obeyed work out not in my presence only, but now much more in my absence, your own salvation with fear and trembling. For it is God which worketh in you both to will and to work, for His good pleasure."[1]

A parallel may be of value in enabling us to gain a clearer impression of Paul's religious and moral personality. In general for the investigation of Paul the comparative method is strongly to be recommended. Paul and Philo, Paul and Seneca, Paul and Epictetus, Paul and James, Paul and Jesus—these are all uncommonly fruitful themes. To-day I should like to compare Paul and Zoilos. Zoilos is not found in any encyclopædia. He has only within the last few years come out

[1] Phil. 2. 12, 13.

AND THE FAITH OF PAUL 259

of the earth again through a papyrus letter of his, which has lately been discovered. Zoilos was a devotee of Sarapis, and his letter, which belongs to the years 258–257 B.C., is directed to Apollonios, the finance minister of the King Ptolemy II Philadelphos of Egypt.

This Zoilos letter is one of the first exact parallels of the letters of Paul in the Greek language: it is an accidentally preserved piece of real propaganda correspondence of an ancient cult. Not propaganda literature, but a reflex of propaganda, in truth an act of propaganda itself, a part of the actual events.

Every ancient missionary cult naturally brought forth such correspondence in large quantities. But this gigantic mass of writings which at one time were sent back and forth between Egypt and the remainder of the territory about the Mediterranean or between Italy and Syria, and in which the visions, the plans, the itineraries of the missionaries, the successes and failures of their efforts and a lively mirroring of the finances of the propaganda are found, is for nearly all cults as good as lost. Only the Christian cult with its gathering and canonising of the letters of Paul has preserved a part of its oldest missionary documents. In the Zoilos letter we have a lost letter of the Sarapis cult which also enables us to understand more correctly the unliterary uniqueness of the apostolic letters.

I have published the Zoilos letter in the fourth edition of my book *Licht vom Osten*, which has just come out in Tübingen (Mohr), and a facsimile of it is printed there.[1]

The text reads as follows :—

To Apollonios greetings from Zoilos the Aspen(d)ian one of the (. . .) (here is a lacuna)
who is presented to you by the friends of the king. It occurred
as I was worshipping before Sarapis interceding for your health and success
with King Ptolemy, that the Sarapis several times
ordered me while sleeping that I should go to you and (give you this)
advice : it is necessary (that you) erect (for him a Sarapis temple)

[1] Pp. 121, 406, 408.
English Edition, Hodder and Stoughton, Ltd.

and a temenos in the Greek quarter near the harbour, and a priest must be placed in charge (and)
sacrifice for you upon the altar. After I had (petitioned the god Sarapis)
that he might relieve me from this (task) he afflicted me with a terrible
sickness so that my life was endangered. But I (promised) in prayer to him that if he
would cure me, I would gladly be obedient to him, and (do) what
was commanded by him. After I had rapidly recovered a man came from Knidos
who tried to build a temple to Sarapis and had brought
the stones for it. Later the god forbade him to build and the man
went away. But when I came to Alexandria and hesitated to
present the matter to you—only in the matter in which you had already given me assurance (did I deal with you)
a relapse came lasting four months, wherefore I could not at once
come to you. It would be well, Apollonios, if you
would obey the god's order, so that Sarapis may be well pleased with you
and that you may become greater and more popular with the king and not to forget the health of your body.
Do not be alarmed at the expense, for it will cost you much.

But therefore it shall be all the more valuable
　　for yourself,
I myself will help to officiate with everything,
　　　　　　　　　　　　　　　Farewell.

On the reverse side :

Note of receipt (in another hand) : Address :
From Zoilos, concerning Sarapis. To Apollonios.
In year 28 on 9 Audnaios
In Berenices
Port,

All the principal parts of the text can be understood. We must, however, seek to place ourselves back in the years 258–257 B.C., at about the time when the first pages of the Septuagint were brought forth in Egypt.

Let us now use this letter for the comparison of Paul and Zoilos. Both similarity and decisive contrast can be observed. Both men consider their propaganda as their holy duty.[1] Paul, like Zoilos, stands under the direct working authority of his Lord, and is led in the serious moments of his life by wisdom

---

[1] Cf. 2 Cor. 9. 12 ; Rom. 15. 16.

AND THE FAITH OF PAUL 263

from above, through command [1] and (as the man from Knidos) through prohibition [2] and he also knows, like the follower of Sarapis, the inescapable divine *must* of such a command.[3] Both dare in prayer to ask for escape from divine burdens, but find out that the higher will is the stronger.[4] Like Zoilos, so Paul is urged in a dream to take an ocean trip,[5] and knows as he does the compelling power of a promise.[6] Like the follower of Sarapis, so the slave of Jesus Christ is visited with a terrible sickness, and Paul recognises, like Zoilos, the suffering as God-willed.[7] Both practised intercession for their cult comrades,[8] and both had to deal seriously with spiritual competitors. Finally in a formal way the mutual unliterary character of both is shown, for instance, in the anacoluthons which mirror the spoken language in their letters.

Sharper, of course, are the contrasts. The power and uniqueness of the apostolic Chris-

---

[1] Gal. 2. 2 ; Acts 22. 18, etc. [2] Acts. 16. 6–7.
[3] Acts 19. 21 ; 1 Cor. 9. 16. [4] 2 Cor. 12. 8 ff.
[5] Acts 16. 9 ff. [6] Acts 18. 18 ; cf. 21. 23 ff.
[7] 2 Cor. 12. 7 ff. [8] Phil. 2. 3, 4.

tian cult is clearly brought out against the background which this Sarapis cult document affords.

First of all, the contrast of the sociological structure is very great. The representative of the Sarapis cult "presented" to the minister of finance has an immediate contact with one of the strongest and richest politicians of his day, and through him closely mediated relations with the court of Ptolemy. The entire letter has as its chief argument what is unexpressed, that the King is thought of as the one who is the protector of the Sarapis cult, and that therefore the founding of a Sarapis temple is the best means of rising in the pleasure of the King. Proportionately a prominent follower of Sarapis does not bother about little matters ; his god entrusts him with commissions which cost—cost indeed so much that even the wealthy Apollonios requires good words to induce him to accept. But even if the finance minister should refuse, gold and stones for the temple would have been there nevertheless.

The tent-maker of Tarsus was not " intro-

AND THE FAITH OF PAUL 265

duced " to anyone. At best he was brought to the state officials as the accused; friendly meetings as with the Governor of Cyprus [1] were accidental. His " relations " were almost exclusively with the propertyless classes.[2] And even his friend from Alexandria, another Apollonios, was *mighty* only in the Scriptures.[3] Court-relations Paul never had; the greetings which he at one time sent *from the house of Cæsar* [4] did not come from princesses and ministers, but from simple slaves of Cæsar, small officials who were possibly working in Ephesus for financial or land interests. Bids for the favour of the court party such as the inspired and disillusioned Zoilos sent, are entirely unknown to the Apostle. If Paul had financial problems to solve, there were no requests for marble, masonry, columns, and statues to consider, for the building mania had not as yet taken hold of the young cult. But building, as we saw, played a great rôle in the imagination of the Apostle, whose Master during His earthly appearance had

[1] Acts 13. 6 ff. [2] 1 Cor. 1. 26 ff.
[3] Acts 18. 24. [4] Phil. 4. 22.

been a builder,[1] and the Apostle also speaks of temples. But with Paul one always thinks of temples "*not made by hands*,"[2] and not paid for in gold, but the body as the temple of the Holy Spirit,[3] the Church as the temple of the living God.[4] And when Paul compares himself with an "architect,"[5] the age of the big Architect-Popes is still far off. But we are grateful to the Apostle for the deep and rich conception of the inner and spiritual edification.[6] Paul, like Zoilos, wrote of financial cares, but he does not present them to a millionaire, but to manual workers who lived in the business and harbour districts of the cities, urging them to save their mites from week to week for their poor comrades in Jerusalem.[7]

Decisive for the historical religious significance of both cults is the deep difference in their ethics. The Sarapis cult as represented by Zoilos, the Aspendian, is in its practical dealings a hedonistic religion. Even though

[1] ὁ τέκτων, Mark 6. 3.　[2] 2 Cor. 5. 1.　[3] 1 Cor. 6. 19.
[4] 1 Cor. 3. 9 ff., 16 ff.; 2 Cor. 6. 16; Eph. 2. 20 ff.
[5] 1 Cor. 3. 10.　　　[6] 1 Cor. 14. 3, 5, 12, 26.
[7] 1 Cor. 16. 1 ff.

AND THE FAITH OF PAUL

sociologically he had acquainted himself with the highest culture of his age, and the art and architecture of the Hellenistic age was at his command, in religion we find here something entirely primitive, really a business "*do ut des*"[1] between man and fetish. Build a temple and your influence with the king will increase ; if not, a severe fever will seize you ! All great religions, even vulgar Christianity, have, in countless instances, closely united their empirical expressions with hedonism, like the religious enthusiasm of Zoilos. They have been Religions of Works. But three hundred years after the letter of Zoilos, different letters from a new cult are sent over the same sea, letters of a religion whose centre of power is Mercy. Though preached to the lowly, the self-renewing energy of the revelation of mercy grasps the great, an Augustine, a Luther. And it will remain the vital core of the Reformations ; for again and again everywhere, even in genuine stock, the savage comes to the surface, and the primitive religion of works—the acting mysticism—

[1] " I give (to you) in order that you may give (to me)."

appears with its original force. The great reformation of Paul, his struggle against justification by works and his zeal for mercy, in practice opposed not only the Jews, but also the cults of the nations. Primitive Christianity was a reacting religion without a tabernacle, but because of the mercy it expressed the apostolic Christ cult had a pre-eminence over the spectacular beauty of its neighbour cults. These cults seemed to be separated from the raw primitive religious customs, because of their fine formal culture. To anyone, however, who has opened their tabernacles, the wild primitive chaos has again been disclosed. One unique element of primitive Christianity is this, that it brings religion in its highest perfection and inwardness near to primitive people, but in unpretentious forms of expression.

In conclusion, I should again like to raise the question, whether I was correct in my general conception of Paul's religion. Is it really right to give up the attempt to select

AND THE FAITH OF PAUL

certain definite doctrines in his teaching, and instead to place at its centre the experience of his communion with Christ? I ask you to allow me to leave these as still unanswered questions. By many, they will still frequently be answered otherwise than I have attempted to answer them, and it is for each to test them for himself, especially by a thorough exegesis of the letters of Paul. I would therefore refer you back to the preliminary questions which I mentioned in the first lecture.

I believe, indeed, that what I have said will be confirmed by the answer to another question. Let us ask, namely, what effect Paul had on succeeding generations? This question is itself of the highest interest, and the varying attempts to answer it are characteristic of varying types of Pauline investigation.

One of the best-known answers to this question is the theory of my venerable colleague, Adolf von Harnack, which I have already mentioned, that Paul found, in the next generation after him, but very small understanding, that only one Christian of the second century understood him—Marcion ; and that he misunderstood him. Here Paul appears like one of the streams of the East that do not reach the ocean, but are swallowed up in the desert.

How is it that this answer has been possible ? It comes, I believe, from that doctrinaire conception of the religion of Paul. Special lines of teaching have been set up as characteristic, especially the teaching of justification by faith.

The great importance of this doctrine in the history of the Reformation, has made it inexpressibly dear to us, and we see it as the banner of battle in the Reformation struggle. From it, therefore, we have got our focus of Paulinism, and have instinctively set up justification as the peculiar Pauline doctrine. If, then, the problem of the effect of Paul on succeeding generations is under discussion, it is naturally asked: How has the Pauline doctrine of justification influenced the thought of the Church ?—Since the traces of the doctrine of justification in the early centuries are small, it is naturally said, Paul was not understood.

What is really the state of things? According to my conception, the doctrine of justification is not the quintessence of Paulinism, but one witness among others to his experience of salvation. Justification is one ancient popular picture-word, alongside many others. Justification is one note which, along with many others—redemption, adoption, etc.—is harmonised in the one chord that testifies to salvation.

That the so-called doctrine of justification is so prominent in Paul's letters, which have come down to us, has less an inner, than an outer, cause. The hard fight against the Judaisers and the Law compelled the Apostle thereto. When, in the second century, the direct struggle with Judaism retired into the background, the necessity for strongly contrasting Justification by Faith with Justification by Works disappeared.

If we wish for a correct answer to the problem of how Paul affected the thought of later generations, we must take for our starting-point communion with Christ. The problem of what effect Paul produced, is a problem of the oldest Christ-mysticism. Thus formulated, the question gains quite another appearance, and the answer is much more positive than the witty saying of Harnack.

When one investigates the effect which Paul had, one must distinguish two sorts of influence which he exerted. The first and greatest influence of the Apostle Paul was the direct influence of his personality, and of the unliterary letters which were the substitute for his personal presence. This personal, unliterary influence continued to be exerted long after his death. Essential elements of his religion remained in the souls of his churches, and have continued from them. We have to realise, that in the second part of the first century there still remained, especially in the western part of Asia Minor, a considerable amount of this personal influence.

To this influence we must, then, add another. This begins at the moment when Paul's letters were gathered together and published, and it became stronger when their place was fixed in the canon. This literary influence of Paul, who from first to last had been un-

AND THE FAITH OF PAUL

literary, naturally depends very much on the exegesis which Pauline letters have received, and it has often been—even up to the present day—not the influence of the real Paul, but the influence of a paper Paul. For example, the impression that Paul made in the nineteenth century was chiefly that of a paper Paul.

It is a thought-provoking matter that we have, from primitive Christianity, one great document which shows the influence of the real Paul, before the collection and publication of his letters. I refer to the Johannine writings. According to my view, the Johannine writings show two things: a lack of knowledge of Paul's letters, and a very considerable understanding of Paul's religion. The ancient tradition of the Church that the author of these writings lived in Asia Minor appears to me to be correct, and I believe that the author, who was a personal disciple of Jesus, lived in the second period of his life for several decades in the atmosphere of Pauline religion.

One might, indeed, throw out the question,

whether perhaps Paul was not dependent on a Johannine Christ-mysticism. Theodor Beza, in his explanation of the allegory of the Vine in John 15., expressed this opinion to his own time. But, apart from other reasons against this, Paul, in Galatians, strongly emphasises his independence of other Apostles, and so I believe we have to take it that the Johannine piety was influenced by Paul, rather than the Pauline by John.

An external auxiliary for the investigation of the influence of Paul, is the formula " in Christ " often mentioned in these lectures. I would warn you indeed against supposing that wherever you find this formula in later times, we have a living influence of Paul. With many, this formula has come to be a mere ornament which they use without thought. In the Johannine writings it is felt and used still, in the full depth of its meaning. John made this thought " in Christ " clear and dear to the whole Christian community, by means of a great popular picture—the allegory of the Vine.[1] It

[1] John 15.

AND THE FAITH OF PAUL 275

might almost be said that this Johannine picture of the Vine is even simpler and more popular than Paul's simile of the body of Christ and its members. I myself grew up in a country where the cultivation of the vine has been carried on for thousands of years, and I always thought that I understood this allegory well, but it became clearer to me when first I saw the vine of western Asia Minor. There everything was more full of life, and under their own sunshine the branches of these vines of Asia Minor seemed to me even more clearly to symbolise the mystery of the communion with Christ.

It is also very worthy of note that John uses the expression " fellowship," [1] a Pauline expression, and that he also knows the mystical use of " the blood of Christ " ; the sixth chapter of John, which offers the greatest difficulty to dogmatic exegesis, is easily understandable by the simple Christian, who also knows with Paul the fellowship of the blood of Christ.[2] In her valuable work, *The*

[1] κοινωνία.
[2] κοινωνία τοῦ αἵματος τοῦ Χριστοῦ, 1 Cor. 10. 16.

Mystic Way, Evelyn Underhill has rightly presented the mystic John after the mystic Paul, and what she there says must not be overlooked by those who are investigating the influence of Paul.

The importance of John is, one may say, that he has amalgamated primitive memories of Jesus with Pauline Christ-mysticism and Christ-cult. At the beginning of his apostolic life is the personal influence of Jesus. He must after that have passed through a long period of the mystical experience of Christ, and then in the evening of his life, in his letters and his Gospel, he created the forms of expression by means of which the Pauline Christ-mysticism became the common property of the Church.

The forms which Paul himself devised were specially personal to Paul himself, and many of them are reflections of himself which cannot be repeated by others. The Johannine expressions of Christ-mysticism are far more general in their appeal, and thereby more world-wide in their influence. It can be said, however, that everywhere where John has influence, Paul is exercising influence through him.

In this also John is a true interpreter and mediator of Pauline mysticism, that he too combines it most closely with ethics, and thus finally saved for Christianity the type of reacting mysticism.

The wider task of indicating the further influence of Pauline mysticism directly and indirectly through John is as attractive as it is comprehensive, but I can naturally not do more than set it before you as a subject for study. Through all the later documents of the New Testament, through the Apostolic Fathers, through the Church Fathers generally, this influence reaches to the middle ages, and right into our own time, and I believe that it has never been completely interrupted.

There is one further question that I should like to put to you, to which I have given some attention, though I have not come to a conclusion upon it: how can we to-day realise for ourselves Pauline Christ-mysticism? I believe for the answering of this question it is not only to theologians that we must look, but also to poets, artists and musicians, and, above all, to all real believers wherever Christianity is found in the world.

GENERAL INDEX

Abba, 54, 63, 86
Adonis-cult, 241
Adoption, 207, 208, 218-219
Afflictions of Christ. See Sufferings.
Agape, 23
Akasha-Chronicle, 156
Anselm, 154, 202
Anthroposophy, 156
Anti-Christ, a parousia of, 21
Apollonios, 259-268
Apollos, 265
Athanasius, 154
Attis-cult, 241
Augustine, 267

Bach, Johann Sebastian, 202, 242
Bang, J. P., 168
Baptism of Jesus, 141
Barnabas, Epistle of, 142
Benedict, 220
Bengel, 37
Bentley, 37
Bernard, 220
Beza, Theodor, 274
Böhlig, Hans, 167
Bover, J. M., 169

Brouwer, A. M., 168
Brun, Lyder, 169
Buddha, 135

Carlyle, 204
Christ, believing on, 204
—— Blood of, 238
——Body of, 239, 251, 253-254
—— Christianity of, 146
—— Communion with, 271
—— crucified, 237-240
—— energy, 189
—— finished work of, 164, 172
—— first-born brother, 251
—— in me, 171, 183, 185, 187, 201
—— Passion of, 236, 241
—— present action of, 164, 172
—— Spirit, 171, 175
Christ-Christianity, 146
Christ-cult, 237, 238, 242, 276
Christ-mysticism, 190, 193, 242, 272, 276
Christologos, 189
Christophoros, 189

GENERAL INDEX

Christos, proper name, 135
Church, Charismatic, 256
—— concept of, 256
Communion. *See* Fellowship.
Cranmer's Bible, 174

Damascus, 181
Deaf-mute, healing of, 66
Death overcome, 228
Delieutraz, Lucien, 167
Doctrinaire view of Paul, 156, 161, 270, 273
Dogmatic method, failure of, 31
Dogmatic misunderstanding of Paul, 180, 207, 240, 270, 273

Elijah, 77
Epictetus, 258
Ethics of Paul, 245–258
Eutychus of Troas, 156
Evangelium, 102, 104 ff

Faith, 65, 66, 94, 178, 203–207
Family of God, 251–253
Father, old Jewish title, 69
Fellowship, 179, 191, 207, 227, 233, 239, 240, 275
Fig-tree, 66, 94, 98–100
Flesh, 190
Forgiveness, 89, 207, 208, 213–214
Francis, 220
Freedom from Law, 228, 229
Freedom of will, 258

Garofalo, 243
Geneva Bible, 174
Genitive, mystic, 177
Gerhard, Johann, 202
Gethsemane, 86
Gnosticism, 38
God, Father, 68, 69 ff., 86, 251
—— forgiveness of (*see* Forgiveness), 87
—— gentle and severe, 91
—— Lord, 68, 69 ff., 90
—— Providence, 87
Goethe, 200
Gospel, English word, 103 ff.
Gospel, of Kingdom, 106
Greek, Attic and Hellenistic, 163

Harnack, Adolf von, 126, 150, 157, 158, 269, 272
Harvey, John W., 48
Hatch and Redpath, 165
Heiler, Friedrich, 47
Heinrici, Georg, 164, 167
Heraclitus, 224
Hexapla, English, 174
Historical method, inadequacy of, 15, 18, 19, 20
Holtzmann, 119
Huck, A., 37

Ignatius (Loyola), 220
" In," preposition, importance of, 164 ff.
In Adam, 172, 226, 227
—— the blood of Christ, 178, 179

GENERAL INDEX

In Christ, 162–174, 187 f., 193, 201, 217, 223, 274
—— the flesh, 172, 226
—— God, 192
—— the Law, 172, 211, 226
—— the Lord (*see* in Christ), 192
—— the name of Christ, 178, 179
—— Sins, 172, 226
—— the (Holy) Spirit, 174, 175
—— Sufferings, 173, 226
—— the world, 173, 226
Irenæus, 150
Isaiah, 80

James, 258
Jeremiah, 80
Jesus' answer to High Priest, 138 ff.
Jesus, approach to, 20, 23
—— Baptism of, 129
—— boy in Temple, 84
—— the carpenter, 27
—— communion with God, 15, 40, 85, 125 *et passim*
—— consciousness of Sonship, 130
—— family of, 27
—— and John the Baptist, 82
—— and Judaism, 48, 49, 70–87, 101
—— Living energy, 20
—— Messiahship, 124, 125, 134

Jesus, Messianic consciousness of, 124, 125, 129, 131, 135, 136, 140, 144–147
—— and old Testament, 83
—— originality of, 149
—— and Paul compared, 258
—— Person of, central, 147
—— Prayers of, 42–68
—— prophetic consciousness of, 126, 137
—— reaction of, to God, 102
—— research about difficult, 15–20
—— revelation of, 22–26
—— similes of, 220
—— and sin, and sinners, 92
—— teaching of, 24, 25, 148
—— tradition of, in Synoptics, 28–39
—— witness of God, 44
—— words of, 17, 34, 36, 41, 44, 88
—— wrote nothing, 16, 28
Johannine Problem, 37
—— Writings, 273
John the Baptist, 38, 77–83, 129
—— Gospel of, 85, 276
Jonah, 137
Justification, 154, 207–212, 271

Kaftan, Julius, 189
Karl, Wilhelm, 166

GENERAL INDEX

Kennedy, H. A. A., 167
Kingdom of God, 48, 101–122, 137, 140

Lagarde, 157
Law, 154, 186, 230
Licht vom Osten, 260
Lord, title of, 69, 90, 136
Love, 60, 228, 249–251
Lundberg, Johannes, 167
Luther, 267
Luther Bible, 173

Manumission, 216
Marana tha, 120
Marcion, 157, 270
Marcionites, 150
Mark, oldest Gospel, 36
Messiah, 81, 82, 134
Messiahship, 123, 124, 132, 139, 140
Messianic consciousness of Jesus, 124, 125, 129, 131, 135, 136, 140, 144–146
—— hope, 74–77
—— idea, Jewish, 133
Moffatt, James, 174
Mommsen, Tycho, 176
Morgan, W., 169
Moulton, James Hope, 163
Mystical excitement, 247 f.
—— experience, 185
—— understanding of Paul, 180
Mysticism, 193–200, 232 n.
—— Acting and Reacting, 196, 197, 246, 267, 268
——and Ethics, 245–257

New Creation, 222 ff.
New Testament in Old, 70
Nietzsche, 157

Oberammergau, 242
Observation, indirect, 39
Of. *See* Genitive.
Of (Jesus) Christ, 162, 177, 178, 202, 204
Old Man, 225
Old Testament, influence of, 71–73
Oral tradition and Gospels, 36
Osiris-cult, 241
Otto, Rudolf, 47

Passion, hymns about, 242
—— Mysticism, 241–244
Paul, Christianity of, 188
—— communion of, with Christ, 153 *et passim*
—— conversion of, 181–187, 225
—— doctrinaire portrait of, 156, 161
—— experience in prayer, 247
—— genitives of, 162, 177
—— influence of, 269–272
—— and the law, 228–233
—— letters of, 16, 17, 159–161
—— a mystic, 192, 193, 199, 246
—— nineteenth-century estimate of, 154

GENERAL INDEX 283

Paul, not personally acquainted with Jesus, 186
—— prepositions of, 162 ff.
—— similes of, 220, 221
Paulinism, 153, 207, 270
Paulus, Rudolf, 168
Peter, confession of, 55, 138
Philo, 85, 258
Prayer of Jesus, 42–68
—— amongst the Jews, 49
—— Liturgical, 53
—— the Lord's, 53
—— of Paul, 247
Prodigal Son, 90
Psalter, 85
Ptolemy II, Philadelphos, 259

Reconciliation, 207, 208, 212–213
Redemption, 154, 207, 208, 214–219
Redpath. *See* Hatch.
Religion of Grace, 196
Religion of Mercy, 267
Religion of Works, 196, 267
Remission, 214
Renewing of mind, 81
Repentance, 112
Righteousness from God, 211

Salvation, 201-221
Salvation, order of, 223
Sarapis, 259 ff.
Schack, Graf, 157
Schettler, Adolph, 177
Schleiermacher, 154
Schmidt, Karl Ludwig, 29

Schmidt, Traugott, 167
Schmitz, Otto, 177, 179, 238
Schmone Esre, 49
Seneca, 85, 258
Septuagint, 165, 175
Sin, 91, 172, 226, 227
Slavery, 215 f.
Social Ethics, 251
Söderblom, Archbishop, 47
Son of David, 140
—— of God, 140
—— of Man, 48, 140–142
Sovereignty of God, 110
Spirit (Holy), 91, 171, 175, 190
Spiritual body, 176, 190
Strachan, Lionel R. M., 203, 204
Sufferings of Christ (*see also* Passion), 235 f.
—— Problem of, 234 ff.
Synonyms of Paul, 161, 207–219, 222
Synoptic Eclecticism, 35

Temple of Herod, 84, 254
—— Simile, 251, 254–257
—— of Solomon 243
Temples unfinished, 254
Thora, 76
Through. *See* Paul, prepositions of.
—— Christ, 162, 176, 180
Tongues, speaking with, 248
Tyndale, 174

Underhill, Evelyn, 276
Union with God, 206

Vine, allegory of, 274 f.

Weber, Hans Emil, 168
Weiss, Bernhard, 167
—— Johannes, 35, 166
Wellhausen, Julius, 150

Wiclif, 174
With (*see also* Paul, prepositions of), 162, 175–177

Zoilos, 258–269

www.ingramcontent.com/pod-product-compliance
Lightning Source LLC
Chambersburg PA
CBHW050341230426
43663CB00010B/1941